THE
GREAT
ACQUISITION

AN INTRODUCTION TO
THE LOUISIANA PURCHASE

BY
PETER J. KASTOR

PREFACE BY
JAMES P. RONDA

Published by:
Lewis and Clark Interpretive Association

Book design, cover illustration and layout by:
Jason Beam, Art Director
Walker Design Group
Great Falls, Montana

This book is published with the assistance of a grant from the Design for Living Fund of the Minneapolis Foundation, through the recommendation of Mr. Peyton J. Huffman.

Published in the United States of America in partnership with the

Lewis and Clark Interpretive Center Foundation
Great Falls, Montana 59405

Lewis and Clark Interpretive Association
4201 Giant Springs Road - Great Falls, Montana 59405
(406) 452-5661
www.lewis-clarkstore.com

TO JOHN AND MAE KASTOR (AKA MOM AND DAD)

PREFACE

James P. Ronda
Barnard Professor of Western American History
The University of Tulsa

In North America's long sweep of history few events have had such transforming power as the Louisiana Purchase. The purchase redrew the political and cultural map of the continent, changed countless lives in unforeseen ways, and eventually reshaped global history. Thomas Jefferson may have sensed as much when he wrote Joseph Priestley in 1804 recalling that "I very early saw that Louisiana was indeed a speck in our horizon which was to burst in a tornado." Some eighty-five years later the distinguished historian Henry Adams made the point in even more forceful terms. "The annexation of Louisiana was an event so portentous as to defy measurement." Virtually every American historian since Adams has reached the same conclusion. The purchase was a defining moment in the history of the United States, the North American continent, and the world. As Bernard DeVoto explained in his classic *Course of Empire*, "the power added to the United States by the Louisiana Purchase is indeed beyond measurement."

Textbooks often recount the Louisiana Purchase story as a drama with a handful of actors. White male diplomats and politicians – Jefferson, Napoleon, Robert R. Livingston, Francois Barbe-Marbois, James Monroe, and James Madison – hold center stage and command our attention. Their words and actions have become our official, national history. But in his masterful new book, historian Peter J. Kastor tells a much larger and more compelling story. It is a story suited to the grand scope and sweep of the purchase itself. Kastor does that by expanding the cast of characters and stretching the stage to global proportions. As he writes, making sense of the purchase "means bringing together a diverse set of people scattered throughout the world." We hear familiar voices like those of William Clark and Meriwether Lewis and then are introduced to new ones like Caddo chief Dehahuit, Louisiana planter Jacques Philippe Villere, and Charles, the reputed leader of a massive 1811 slave revolt in New Orleans. Kastor skillfully uses those voices and lives to illuminate the complexities of race, politics, and imperial geography. The events that led to the purchase and those that flowed from it were not inevitable in their courses and consequences. Always aware of the twists and turns in American history, Peter Kastor has given us a superb guide to the West as suspect terrain, a world where the unexpected is up every trail and down each river. Based on careful archival research and informed by the best current scholarship, this book is a major contribution to our understanding of the early republic and its march west.

Acknowledgments

I have an abundance of thanks to offer. This book began with an offhand comment. In the summer of 1993 I spoke at the annual meeting of the Lewis and Clark Trail Heritage Foundation. In a conversation with Ella Mae Howard following that talk, I lamented the absence of a short book that explained the Louisiana Purchase. Ella Mae got me to put my money where my mouth was. She made the project happen, coordinating discussion between Central Virginia and Central Montana, two very different ends of Lewis and Clark's transcontinental path.

What followed was a project that had to compete for time with my dissertation at the University of Virginia. I could engage in both tasks because I had a secret weapon: the Papers of James Madison. The editors provided access to their collection and offered constant advice. I simply could not have completed this manuscript—or the dissertation—in a timely manner without their support. Once I began writing, this manuscript moved through various incarnations, each of which required the assistance and patience of a variety of people. The first to read the manuscript—Robert Guffin, J.C.A. Stagg, and Andy Trees—provided vital assistance in moving my vague ideas to a more cohesive form. At the Lewis and Clark Interpretative Association, Ella Mae Howard read through several drafts and distilled the comments of her colleagues. Katrina Stark, the Association's executive director, became my chief contact, remaining cheerful and tremendously helpful throughout the process. In the final stages, Jim Ronda signed on to read two versions of this book. A magnificent writer in his own right as well as an outstanding historian of the North American West, Jim offered thorough evaluation and constructive criticism.

This book is dedicated to my parents. This is appropriate for my first book, for no one else has been more enthusiastic or supportive. I have also benefited from acquiring another source of support, my wife, Jami Ake, whom I met right before starting this project. Finally, I want to thank my son, Sam, who is not yet old enough to read these words. Born in the spring 2001, just as I prepared the final stages of this project, his endless humor has provided me with endless happiness.

TABLE OF CONTENTS

INTRODUCTION
THE LETTERS

In March 1803 James Madison wrote a letter. The secretary of state's letters carried considerable weight. Few people disputed that Madison was the second most powerful man in the federal government, superseded only by his friend, Thomas Jefferson. President Jefferson turned to his secretary of state for advice. By contrast, Jefferson neither trusted nor respected his vice president, Aaron Burr, who had few official responsibilities and did not enjoy great influence within the cabinet.

There was more to Madison's power than his influence on the president, however. The structure of the American government guaranteed the secretary of state had unrivaled authority. Then, as now, the State Department directed the nation's foreign relations. But the secretary of state also acted as the President's liaison with the nation's governors. Perhaps more important, the secretary of state had direct charge over the nation's far-flung territories, a responsibility which gave him control over a geography larger than any of the states.

In the spring of 1803 Madison wielded all his power with a small staff working from a cramped headquarters in an unfinished capital. Washington, D.C. had served as the nation's capital for less than three years. The struggling town was a far cry from the cosmopolitan cities of New York and Philadelphia that had hosted the federal government during the 1790's. The State and War Departments shared a single building. Madison directed the State Department with seven clerks and a single messenger who faced the daunting task of traversing the muddy streets of Washington and the Tiber River, which separated the Capitol Building from the cluster of offices surrounding the President's

House (the term people used for The White House).[1]

Madison spent much of his time in conference with Jefferson, and the letter was their collaboration. It was addressed to Robert R. Livingston and James Monroe. Livingston was in Paris, serving as American minister to France. Monroe had recently been appointed minister plenipotentiary—or special envoy—to assist Livingston, but was still in the United States. With Monroe preparing to board the ship that would take him across the Atlantic, Madison believed he faced his last chance to influence events in France.

The lengthy letter concerned itself with one topic: the American quest to secure control of the Mississippi River. As Madison explained to the diplomats, "the object in view is to procure by just and satisfactory arrangements, a Cession to the United States, of New Orleans, and of West and East Florida." Madison told Monroe and Livingston to be prepared to haggle and engage in horse-trading to achieve this goal. They could buy other land from France so long as it was a temporary expedient that would create the conditions for American acquisition of the vital territory where the Mississippi River leads to the Gulf of Mexico.[2]

In the middle of his instructions Madison included a draft of a treaty he hoped Monroe and Livingston would press upon the French. In it, the United States would buy a small area of land for a small price. Although he never used the term, what Madison described was the administration's version of a "Louisiana Purchase" that included no land west of the Mississippi. Instead, the United States would consolidate its possessions east of the Mississippi by acquiring New Orleans and the Floridas (a vague term which referred to the Gulf Coast and the Florida Peninsula).

Madison concluded his letter by stating, "These instructions, tho as full as they could be conveniently made, will necessarily leave much to your discretion." He could not imagine how much discretion his diplomats would assume. A series of letters eventually reached

---

[1] *PJM-SS1*, xxiii; Young, *The Washington Community 1800-1828*
[2] James Madison to Robert R. Livingston and James Monroe, 2 March 1803, *PJM-SS4*, 364-78.

Washington that told of a far different Louisiana Purchase than the one Jefferson and Madison had envisioned.

The first of those letters came from Livingston and Monroe. Written on May 13, 1803, the letter announced that "we have the pleasure to transmit to you...a Treaty which we have concluded with the French Republic for the Purchase & Cession of Louisiana."[3] This letter included a document entitled "Treaty Between the United States of America and the French Republic," as well as three additional "Conventions" governing the details and implementation of that treaty. It was the agreement described in these documents—and not the one detailed by Madison—that became known as the Louisiana Purchase. In this treaty France would cede all its territory in North America for nearly fifteen million dollars.

This was not what Jefferson and Madison sought, nor was it necessarily what they wanted. But there was little the administration could do. By the end of the year the United States was struggling to make its sovereignty over the Louisiana Purchase into a reality.

Just what the Louisiana Purchase would mean was anybody's guess. The range of attitudes became clear in the second letter to reach Madison's desk. The author was William C.C. Claiborne. Six months after Madison sent his instructions and four months after Livingston and Monroe informed the administration of the Louisiana Purchase, Claiborne was packing his bags. Jefferson had appointed Claiborne one of two commissioners to oversee the transfer of Louisiana to the United States. The twenty-eight-year-old governor of the Mississippi Territory was apprehensive as he prepared to move himself, his wife, and their young daughter to New Orleans. On September 29, Claiborne's party reached the small border town of Natchez, the last stop before descending the Mississippi River to New Orleans. As he gathered what little information he could about the residents of Louisiana, Claiborne wrote Jefferson that the "present Government of Louisiana is a Despotism, partly Civil, partly Military, and in some degree ecclesiastical."[4] He predicted that the Louisiana

---

[3] Livingston and Monroe to Madison, 13 May 1803, *PJM-SS4*, 601.

Purchase would create unprecedented demands on the federal government.

The next letter came from Cahokia, a rough frontier settlement on the eastern banks of the Mississippi in what is now Illinois. A thousand years before, Cohokia had been the site of the largest city in North America, a massive settlement that the Indians eventually abandoned for reasons that remain a mystery to this day. On December 19, 1803, Captain Meriwether Lewis told Jefferson, his mentor and benefactor, about the expedition he would soon lead up the Missouri River. Lewis wrote, "on my arrival...I made a selection of a sufficient number of men...and made a requisition on the Contractor to cause immediately and adequate deposit of provision." Lewis assured the president he was on his way to a successful expedition.[5]

A fourth communiqué did not go directly to Washington, nor did it begin as a letter. It was a speech by the Caddo chief, Dehahuit, in September 1806. The Caddo Indians lived in an area that now overlaps the borders of Arkansas, Louisiana, and Texas, land claimed by both the United States and Spain in 1806. Instead of looking west to Louisiana—as Monroe, Livingston, Claiborne, and Lewis had done in 1803—Dehahuit looked east to the United States. The American delegation wrote down Dehahuit's speech and sent it to Madison. "My words resemble the words my forefathers have told me they used to receive from the French in ancient times," Dehahuit explained. "If your nation has purchased what the French formerly possessed, you have purchased the country that we occupy, and we regard you in the same light as we did them." Dehahuit wanted the Americans to understand that if they intended to claim Louisiana, they had better consider what Indians had to say.[6]

These four communications each indicated a distinct vision of the Louisiana Purchase. Each was fundamentally different from the acquisition that Jefferson and Madison wrote about in their March 1803 letter. To Monroe and Livingston, the Louisiana Purchase was a matter of high diplomacy, with a fate decided by negotiators at the

---

[4] William C.C. Claiborne to Thomas Jefferson, 29 September 1803, *Jefferson Papers*, Reel 47.
[5] Meriwether Lewis to Jefferson, 19 December 1803, Jackson, ed., *Letters of the Lewis and Clark Expedition*, I: 145.
[6] Dehahuit to Claiborne, 5 September 1806, *Claiborne Letterbooks*, IV: 4.

center of power. To Claiborne it was a place filled with a population in need of a new government. To Lewis it was an unknown country waiting to be explored. To Dehahuit it was home, the future of which was uncertain.

This book offers an introduction to the Louisiana Purchase, and provides the reasons why people like Monroe and Livingston, Madison, Claiborne, Lewis, and Dehahuit would all interpret the same treaty in such different terms. The Louisiana Purchase extended American dominion to encompass the Mississippi Delta, the Great Plains, and the Rockies. Far from a simple transfer of land, the treaty came in the wake of complex international developments and unleashed unpredicted repercussions. The Louisiana Purchase stimulated controversy, crisis, and dynamic change. Rather than resolve diplomatic affairs, the Louisiana Purchase served as the catalyst that unsettled the Americas long after 1803.

The small cession that Madison and Jefferson sought in the spring of 1803 is an indication of the way Americans understood their nation and its future. By contrast, the treaty Livingston and Monroe negotiated doubled the size of the United States and fundamentally changed the way Americans thought.

Understanding the Louisiana Purchase must begin not with answers but with questions:

Why did it happen? Why did the French government sell its holdings in North America? Likewise, why did the United States agree to spend $15 million for land American policymakers had not sought?

How did it happen? How was the United States able to secure such a massive land deal at such a low cost? How did the United States hope to convert a European colony into an American province?

Finding answers to these questions must start by remembering that the world in which the Louisiana Purchase occurred was fundamentally different from our own. Even the name—Louisiana—was confusing because it referred to three separate entities. The

Louisiana that is the subject of this book included the entire territory purchased by the United States in 1803. There was also the State of Louisiana, which was to join the union in 1812 with much the same borders it has today. Third, there was the Territory of Louisiana, which referred to everything *north* of the State of Louisiana. And then there is one final complication: all of this geography was subject to dispute. Exactly what constituted Louisiana generated international disagreement for years after 1803.

But making sense of Louisiana entails more than understanding the geography. The story extends well beyond the boundaries of Louisiana to include men and women in the eastern United States, the Caribbean, Spanish America, and Europe. These people—together with their talents and foibles, ambitions and failures, families and homes—help explain why the culture of Louisiana took shape the way it did and why it became part of the United States.

The people in this story include a number of familiar names: Thomas Jefferson and James Madison (who occupy center stage in this narrative), Napoleon Bonaparte, Meriwether Lewis, and William Clark. The story of Louisiana also includes a cast of less familiar characters. Peter Custis, Thomas Freeman, and Zebulon Pike all attempted to create a cohesive picture of Louisiana by exploring the new American frontier. William Claiborne devoted almost a decade-and-a-half to governing Louisiana. Dehahuit and other Indian leaders concluded that the Louisiana Purchase created new dangers as well as new opportunities. Jacques Philippe Villeré embodied the aspirations of white residents of Louisiana, who, like Dehahuit, saw a range of threats and possibilities. The biographies of these men help explain the process by which the United States acquired and then consolidated its hold on Louisiana. There were thousands of other individuals—white settlers, Indians, slaves, and free people of color—who found their lives disrupted by the Louisiana Purchase. While it is impossible to reconstruct detailed biographies of these anonymous individuals, understanding the dynamics of these groups is crucial to understanding the Louisiana Purchase.

Making sense of the Louisiana Purchase also entails the difficult task of forgetting. It is almost impossible to forget that the United States would extend clear to the Pacific Ocean. It is tempting to see a hint of Manifest Destiny, the impulse for expansion that reached full force in the 1840s. But in the first decades after independence from Great Britain, few Americans had such ambitions. Although a highly vocal group did call for unchecked expansion, this group was a minority in most public debates. Instead, many worried that expansion would do more harm than good.

The treaty that Monroe and Livingston signed lies at the center of this narrative, and the narrative is divided in two parts. The first examines the developments in Europe and the Americas that precipitated France's decision to cede Louisiana to the United States. I begin with the residents of Louisiana and the United States. It is necessary to know something of the history of European settlement in the Mississippi Valley, as well as the reasons why Louisiana concerned people in the United States. After describing the uncertainty North Americans felt as they contemplated what would become of Louisiana, I shift to Paris, where the leadership of Revolutionary France dictated the terms of the Louisiana Purchase.

The second part of the book discusses events after 1803, as the United States attempted to consolidate its sovereignty over Louisiana. It would be easy to end the story in 1803. Most histories of the time often do, as if the acquisition of Louisiana ended when diplomats signed the treaty. It was not until the 1820's, however, that people could confidently claim that the questions unleashed by the Louisiana Purchase were answered. Where would Louisiana end? Would whites, Indians, or slaves wield power? What would be the relationship between Louisiana and the United States? These questions were hardly settled in 1803. This book focuses on how the United States acquired Louisiana and what that acquisition meant in the decades that followed.

A matter of critical importance to this book is my own effort to differentiate the world of the Louisiana Purchase from our own. I emphasize this point because too often we assume that the actors in history seem "real" only when they say or do the things we say or do today. People in the late-eighteenth and early-nineteenth centuries often understood their world in terms that would seem entirely alien for us, and their actions—which now seem ludicrous—often made sense given their circumstances.

People on both sides of the Atlantic saw the Louisiana Purchase as the source of unprecedented change, unparalleled opportunity, and considerable danger. The Louisiana Purchase played no small part in generating those changes, opportunities, and dangers. It also brought into stark relief a series of profound developments occurring nationwide and throughout the world. Few people saw those developments coming. They were not clairvoyant and often unleashed changes unimaginable to them.

Chapter One
"A Great Struggling Town"

That Louisiana would become the object of so much attention would have struck most seventeenth and eighteenth-century observers as perplexing, if not amusing. In a New World filled with thriving European colonies, Louisiana remained for many years an anonymous outpost, a backward, almost deserted settlement. Indeed, the early history of Louisiana testifies to the difficulties of colonization, affected as it was by international war, racial conflict, and the vagaries of European imperial economies.

Before Europeans arrived, the Mississippi Valley was a crowded and prosperous place. The eastern banks of the Upper Mississippi in what is now Illinois had been home to the massive Indian settlement at Cahokia. In the Lower Mississippi Valley, the Choctaw, Kaddohadacho, and Natchez Indians—some of them descendants of the people who had abandoned Cahokia—created elaborate systems of diplomacy and trade. Although the Spaniard Hernando de Soto led an expedition through the Lower Mississippi Valley in 1542, regular contact did not follow him. Instead, Europeans would only make occasional trips through the region during the sixteenth and seventeenth centuries. Indians in the Mississippi Valley certainly knew about Europeans, but they were rarely on the scene, and other, more horrifying developments demanded the Indians' attention. Of much greater importance was the sudden and devastating arrival of European diseases, which eradicated whole villages. Indians often distinguished between the diseases and the Europeans themselves, because physical contact was not a necessity for contagion.

The way European diseases devastated the Indian population in the Mississippi Valley confused Indians and Europeans alike and gave Europeans a skewed notion of Indian settlement patterns. When Europeans visited the region at the end of the seventeenth century, they encountered Indians, but only a mere fraction of the population of the previous century. The result was that Europeans tended to treat the Mississippi Valley as a vacant region, a conclusion that was logical but not accurate.[7]

The French saw the Mississippi River as an important highway, but did not consider it a particularly attractive home. Although the Spanish were the first permanent Europeans to explore the area, the French built the first European settlements, and for very practical reasons. The Mississippi River offered a rapid passage from the French colony of Canada to the Gulf of Mexico and, in turn, to the Atlantic. France could foster settlements further inland, far from the maritime provinces of eastern Canada. Some enthusiastic French and French Canadian boosters believed the Mississippi Valley offered a chance for personal advancement and a way to expand the French holdings in North America.

These visions of a prosperous Canada and personal glory—rather than a deep interest in the Lower Mississippi Valley—inspired René Robert Cavalier, Sieur de La Salle, to command an expedition down the length of the Mississippi in 1682. His team was a mix of thirty-three European men joined by thirty Indian men and women. His charter from the French government was a modest one: to explore the Upper Mississippi Valley and negotiate with the Indians near French settlements on the Great Lakes. La Salle was unwilling to be shackled by these commands, however, and chose instead to descend the length of the Mississippi.

La Salle was a loyal Frenchman and a shrewd leader with more than his share of entrepreneurial aspirations. As a young man, for

---

[7] For the effects of European disease on the Indians of North America, see Axtell, *Beyond 1492;* Dobyns, *Their Number Become Thinned;* Ramenofsky, *Vectors of Death;* Thornton, *American Indian Holocaust and Survival;* White, *The Middle Ground,* 40-1.

Illustration: Jean Baptiste Michel Le Bouteaux, *View of the Campe of the Concession of Monseigneur Law at New Biloxi, Coast of Louisiana* (1710), Courtesy of the Edward E. Ayer Collection, Newberry Library, Chicago. Color plate, page 167.

example, he had secured a monopoly over the fur trade near Lake Ontario from King Louis XIV. It was with a combination patriotic fervor and wise flattery for the king that La Salle named the new possession "this country of Louisiana." The name stuck.[8]

Convinced that the Lower Mississippi Valley would enable France to control the length of the river and, in turn, expand French commerce and power in the Americas, King Louis XIV endorsed subsequent surveying expeditions.[9] The first settlement in the Lower Mississippi Valley at Biloxi, however, occurred by accident. When a twenty-seven-year-old Canadian named Pierre Le Moyne, Sieur d'Iberville, led an expedition to the Lower Mississippi in 1699, he had no intention of creating a permanent European presence. When his attempt to reconnoiter the Gulf Coast fell behind schedule, Iberville was forced to build shelter. Since "the little provisions I had left would not permit us to stay longer on the coast," d'Iberville explained, "it was necessary to establish a post quickly."[10]

---

[8] Muhlstein, *La Salle,* 156-7.
[9] Muhlstein, *La Salle,* 210.
[10] Williams, ed., *Iberville's Gulf Journals,* 89. See also Johnson, "Colonial New Orleans," in *Creole New Orleans,* 29.

"A GREAT STRUGGLING TOWN"

Such haphazard settlement became the norm in Louisiana. d' Iberville himself soon lost interest, convinced that greater glory and wealth lay elsewhere. He left little trace of his presence because members of this first surveying expedition—mostly ruffians and jailbirds—were incapable of successful farming. [11] d' Iberville himself died in 1706 of Yellow Fever while leading an assault on Cuba, and few French settlers chose Louisiana.

During the first half of the eighteenth century, rumors of an unpleasant climate and violent Indians dissuaded French settlers. The French government tired of the expenses that came with the colony, and for a brief period allowed a private company created by Scotsman John Law to run Louisiana. Ships from Europe brought a steady trickle of newcomers, but few had the experience or gumption to establish a successful colony. Only through misleading enticements, military service, and slavery did France sustain a colony in Lower Mississippi. Among the vessels that reached Louisiana in 1718 was *L'Aurore*. French seamen drove nearly two hundred slaves from her hold, the first large collection of African slaves to join the Europeans and Indians in the Lower Mississippi. *L'Aurore's* human cargo quickly became a tide of almost 6,000 slaves reaching Louisiana from 1720 to 1750. French planters welcomed the forced laborers, believing that African slaves would be the only way to create a large population in Louisiana.[12] Also in 1718, d' Iberville's brother, the governor of Louisiana—also named Pierre, but known as Sieur Bienville—decided to move the colonial capital from Biloxi to a small bulge of land on the eastern bank of the Mississippi. He named the settlement New Orleans.

While British, French, and Spanish colonies throughout the Americas began to thrive at the beginning of the eighteenth century, both New Orleans and the larger region called Louisiana stagnated. At the same time European settlements like Philadelphia, Montreal, and Mexico City were growing into boisterous cities, New Orleans

---

[11] Usner, *Indians, Settlers, & Slaves in a Frontier Exchange Economy*, 31-3.
[12] Allain, *"Not Worth a Straw,"* 85-8; Gwendolyn Midlo Hall, "The Formation of Afro-Creole Culture," in *Creole New Orleans*, 70; Usner, *Indians, Settlers, & Slaves in a Frontier Exchange Economy*, 80.

remained a small town. The French proved incapable of harvesting enough crops even for their own survival, let alone for export. Louisiana's Indians provided food and supplies to stave off the colony's destruction. As encouraging as this may sound, Europeans and Indians were not always good neighbors. Louisiana remained unattractive to most European settlers because Indians repeatedly staged violent reprisals against European trespasses on Indian land. Throughout the eighteenth century, the Indians concluded that Europeans were both violent and unreliable, and white settlers felt vulnerable to both Indian attack and slave revolt.[13]

To the leaders in Paris, the Lower Mississippi was a strategic outpost rather than a center for migration and trade. Control over the Lower Mississippi Valley provided the means to safeguard French trade down the Mississippi against France's chief European rivals, Britain and Spain. So France invested enough resources to sustain the colony, but not enough to fuel its growth. The colony's existence remained precarious. French leaders were concerned about the periodic warfare between European settlers and Indians within Louisiana, but they considered France's struggle for supremacy among its European neighbors a more important conflict.

The competing imperial ambitions in Europe exploded into open warfare in 1754. France and Britain were the chief protagonists, with the Spanish and numerous Indian tribes joining the fray. The Seven Years War—also called the French and Indian War—ranged from vicious skirmishes in the backwoods of Virginia to the confrontation of armies in Canada to titanic sea battles in the Mediterranean. The most famous veteran of that conflict was a young member of the Virginia gentry named George Washington, who learned about British military tactics first-hand while fighting alongside English regulars against French and Indian soldiers.

The Seven Years War did not reach down the Mississippi River into the French settlement of Louisiana, but it was the first in a series of international events that transformed life in the Lower Mississippi.

---

[13] Usner, *Indians, Settlers, & Slaves in a Frontier Exchange Economy*, 31-3.

In 1759, the British captured Quebec and soon consolidated control over Canada. With Canada gone, there was little reason for the French to keep Louisiana. This strategic reality was confirmed in 1763 when France, meeting with other European nations at the end of the war, ceded Louisiana to Spain.

Thus began a difficult transition for the people of Louisiana. After some initial attempts to satisfy the concerns of Louisiana's European settlers, the Spanish imposed commercial and political restrictions. In 1768 a gathering of Louisiana planters expelled the first Spanish governor, who fled one step ahead of angry settlers and felt safe only when he was aboard a Spanish ship heading for Havana.[14] The planters' rebellion did not occur in a vacuum. They were well aware of similar events to the east, where British colonists reacted violently to the Stamp Act. But where the British government acceded to the demands of its colonists, the Spanish rushed troops from Cuba and crushed the uprising in Louisiana. A dozen men were arrested, half of whom were dispatched to a Cuban prison and released only after promising that they never return to Louisiana. Five others were executed by firing squad and the sixth, Joseph Roy de Villeré, was found dead in his prison cell.[15]

The Spanish never explained how Villeré died, but his family claimed guards murdered Villeré at the behest of Spanish officials. Villeré's widow fled New Orleans with her two young children, finding sanctuary on the plantation of a family friend. She arranged passage to Saint-Domingue, a French colony in the Caribbean outside Spanish jurisdiction. She remained in this self-imposed exile, dying in Saint-Domingue in 1782. Her son, Jacques Philippe, asked Spain for permission to return to Louisiana. The Spanish government permitted his repatriation, but only after young Jacques swore allegiance to Spain. Jacques picked up where his father left off as a planter and politician, albeit without the rebellious tendencies. He built a thriving plantation and served in a variety of public offices. But he never forgot what the Spanish did to his family, nor did he stop dreaming of a day when the

---

[14] Brasseaux, *Denis-Nicolas Foucault and the New Orleans Rebellion of 1768;* Moore, *Revolt in Louisiana,* 12-14, 42-59, 11-56, 147-64; Villeré, *Jacques Philippe Villeré,* 13-8.
[15] Din and Harkins, *The New Orleans Cabildo,* 48-9; Texada, *Alejandro O'Reilly and the New Orleans Rebels.*

residents of Louisiana would control their own destinies.[16]

Villeré's behavior was common to Louisiana's planters. White settlers did not renew their challenge to Spanish authority and stifled whatever animosity they harbored toward the new regime. As Louisiana's economy began to blossom, planters like Jacques de Villeré found themselves increasingly wealthy. Louisiana's population also began to increase. For its first half-century, Louisiana's white and black populations only grew through the constant influx of newcomers from Europe and Africa. A generation later, enough children had survived the rigors of colonial life to produce a colony growing of its own accord. These native-born residents were called "creoles," a term applied throughout the New World to the children of immigrants from Europe and Africa. While creoles in other regions became known as Mexicans or Pennsylvanians or Canadians, the descendants of French and African immigrants to Louisiana made the term their own. To this day, the term has special meaning in Louisiana.

The Creoles soon had company. Ironically, it was the collapse of the old French empire that provided the greatest boon to Louisiana's population. As the British took charge of Canada, the old residents of Acadia—French Catholics living in the Northeastern corner of Canada—soon found themselves outnumbered by Protestant immigrants from the British Isles. Whether for religious or economic reasons, Acadians traded the cold temperatures and rocky soil of the Northeast for the swampy lands of southern Louisiana, where they eventually became known as "Cajuns." In the 1790's Frenchmen fleeing the violence of the Revolution in France and the French Caribbean joined the Cajuns in Spanish Louisiana.

The burgeoning population was not limited to whites. Though the slave trade dwindled in the last years of French rule, the Spanish helped orchestrate a dramatic increase in the importation of human property. These Africans joined an existing population of slaves who, like white Louisianians, were having children of their own. By 1800,

---

[16] Villeré, *Jacques Philippe Villeré*, 13-21.

"A GREAT STRUGGLING TOWN"

"Creole" was no longer an adequate term for the polyglot population of Louisiana. The combination of Creoles together with newcomers from Europe, the Caribbean, and Africa created a population of "Louisianians."

The growth in slavery also helps explain why white Louisianians continued to accept Spanish rule. Periodic slave revolts confirmed the fear of white planters. Spanish officials provided protection in the form of Spanish troops. Whatever their feelings about the Spaniards in charge, white Louisianians would not consider challenging the status quo.[17]

As whites succeeded in providing for themselves, the old equilibrium between Indians, European settlers, and African slaves during the first half of the eighteenth century collapsed. The growing white population began to covet Indian lands. Indians found themselves unable to hold back the power of white settlers and were divided over how to respond. Increasingly compressed from all sides, the Indians of the Lower Mississippi Valley began to fight for control of their own land.[18]

Similar developments were occurring in the Upper Mississippi Valley. European trappers and frontiersmen were spreading throughout the Eastern Plains, establishing trading posts on the Mississippi approximately halfway between the Great Lakes and the Gulf of Mexico. They, too, were predominantly French, whether born in Europe or in Canada. One outpost, Ste. Genevieve, was a small settlement. The nearby town of St. Louis was even less consequential. Nevertheless, the population of whites was growing as was the concern of the Indians.

The Spanish, too, were inviting citizens of the new nation to the east—the United States—to migrate into Upper Louisiana. The number of Americans remained small, but, together with the French-speaking residents of St. Genevieve and St. Louis, they outnumbered those few Spanish officials or settlers who came to Louisiana.[19]

---

[17] Hall, *Africans in Colonial Louisiana*, 344-74; Lachance, "The Politics of Fear," 177-84.
[18] Usner, *Indians, Settlers, & Slaves in a Frontier Exchange Economy*, 230.
[19] Ekberg, *Colonial Ste. Genevieve*; Foley, *The Genesis of Missouri*, 41-6.

Leaders, in both Madrid and the United States, drew a distinction between Upper and Lower Louisiana. These terms described two different worlds rather than one distinct colony. Lower Louisiana included the increasingly crowded society of planters, merchants, and slaves of the Lower Mississippi Valley. Upper Louisiana was home to a more dispersed population inhabiting a landscape still dominated by Indians. Increasingly, each had to be managed differently.[20]

The Spanish were content to let Louisianians make their own choices as long as they did not challenge Spanish authority. Spanish customs and Spaniards themselves became a vital part of Louisiana life, but the French colonial past was always visible. The Spanish did not attempt to impose their own language onto the Louisianians. Most white residents spoke French, whether the formal language of Paris or the dialects of the Creoles, Cajuns, and Caribbeans. Their homes revealed the ongoing influence of the architecture of France and the French Caribbean, and many of the customs that emerged under French rule remained in place.[21]

Despite the developing culture, the future of Louisiana remained in doubt. When Jacques Pitot, an expatriate Frenchman who settled in the United States, visited the Lower Mississippi Valley at the turn of the nineteenth century, he concluded that "more than any other colony, Louisiana has experienced the extent to which a government could go in tying its resources." Another French traveler named Berquin-Duvallon made the disdainful observation that New Orleans "deserves rather the name of a great struggling town than of a city." Still, both authors believed that, under the right circumstances, the colony might prosper. Pitot predicted, "Louisiana will soon prove that the combined advantages of its resources can overcome the most malevolent authority" and Berquin-Duvallon qualified his comments with the caveat that "it must however be acknowledged that New-Orleans is destined by nature to be one of the principal cities of North America."[22]

The New Orleans that Berquin-Duvallon described consisted of

---

[20] Foley, *The Genesis of Missouri*, 80-121.
[21] Din and Harkins, *The New Orleans Cabildo*, 7-8; Johnson, "Colonial New Orleans," in *Creole New Orleans*, 47-51.
[22] Pitot, *Observations on the Colony of Louisiana*, 2; Berquin-Duvallon, *Travels in Louisiana and the Floridas*, 35.

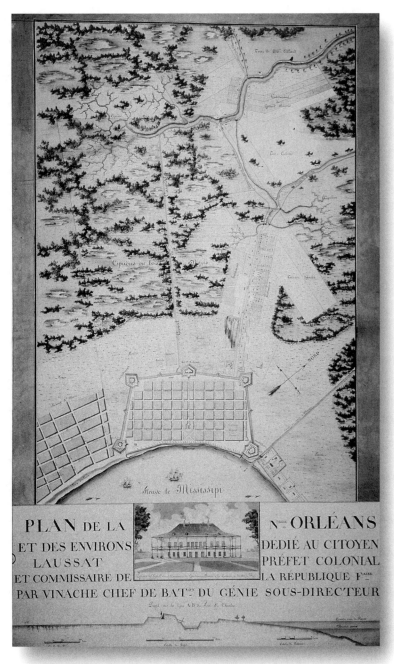

Joseph Antoine Vinache, *Plan de la Nouvelle Orléans et des Environs Dedié au Citoyen Laussat Préfet Colonial et Commissaire de la Republique Francaise* Courtesy of the Historic New Orleans Collection, accession no. 1987.65. Color plate, page 168.

approximately 8,000 residents, split almost in half between people of European and African ancestry. Within these two groups, however, were numerous divisions. As much as any place in North America, New Orleans testified to the fact that American cities emerged from a wealth of cultures. French, Spanish, British, German, American, Caribbean, African, and Indian influences all came together. The way people worked and even the food they ate attested to this variety. Much of the cuisine that is now such a hallmark of Louisiana was the product of intercultural exchange. "Creole" and "Cajun," the two terms people most often use to distinguish Louisiana cooking, does not do justice to the breadth of influences in the Lower Mississippi Valley.

Surrounding New Orleans were increasingly profitable plantations. Only the wealthiest of Louisiana's rural residents enjoyed plantation life, however. Most white families were crowded into rudimentary homes. Lower Louisiana was as much an African society as it was a French one. Plantations that might have only a single family of a half-dozen whites were often the home of dozens of black families. The majority of the residents of rural Lower Louisiana were enslaved, most of them living in rough shacks. Culture ran both ways. Slaves combined their own customs with those of their French masters, and whites adapted African methods for raising crops and cooking food.[23]

It is, of course, tempting to use the writings of men like Pitot and Berquin-Duvallon as the best measure of Louisiana. After all, they were there at the time, and, as travelers, they brought an outsider's perspective. Nonetheless, their comments cannot be taken at face value. While they were correct in their observations that Louisiana's economy lagged behind that of other European colonies, their inclination to blame problems on the Spanish was not entirely valid. Under Spanish rule Louisiana's population as well as its economy had begun to grow. How then do we account for their attacks on Spanish imperial policy? Their attitudes were most likely rooted, at least in

---

[23] Usner, *Indians, Settlers, & Slaves in a Frontier Exchange Economy,* 204-10.

       "A GREAT STRUGGLING TOWN"

part, in their own ethnic chauvinism. Both Frenchmen by birth, they were only the latest in a series of Europeans to accuse the Spanish of decadence and corruption. Both men had other models of culture, either in France or in America.

Pitot and Berquin-Duvallon were also writing at a moment when Revolutions in Britain and France had made politics and empire seem particularly important. The rival monarchies of France, Britain, and Spain had determined affairs in Louisiana during the seventeenth and eighteenth centuries. In the early nineteenth century, it was the revolutionary regimes in France and the United States that would settle Louisiana's fate.

CHAPTER TWO
REVOLUTION

While residents of Louisiana faced the realities of life under the changing governance of the French and Spanish empires in the West, Thomas Jefferson and James Madison were struggling with the governance of a newly created nation in the East. Despite the distance that separated them, people on both sides of the Mississippi were asking similar questions. When Louisianians rose up against the Spanish in 1768, for example, they mirrored the activities of British colonists in North America, who had just completed their own showdown with the British Parliament over the Stamp Act. During the last two decades of the eighteenth century, Louisianians were asking what it meant to be Spanish subjects. Similiarly people in the United States were arguing about what it meant to be American. Some people also became convinced that Louisiana was crucial to the survival of the United States.

Americans were talking about Louisiana's importance before they had even secured their independence. First among these were Jefferson and Madison. In 1781, while the fledging United States was still at war with Great Britain, Jefferson claimed that "the *Missisipi* will be one of the principal channels of future commerce."[1] Madison reached a similar conclusion in 1784. He saw bumper crops and increasing prosperity for western settlers, and he informed Jefferson that "nothing can delay such a revolution with regd. to our staple, but an impolitic & perverse attempt in Spain to shut the mouth of the Miss[issipp]i. agst. the trade of the inhab[itant]s."[2]

---

[1] Jefferson, *Notes on the State of Virginia*, in Peterson, ed., *The Portable Thomas Jefferson*, 35. See also Jefferson to Thomas Pleasants, 8 May 1786, Boyd, IX: 472.
[2] Madison to Jefferson, 20 August 1784, *PJM-8*, 1-4.

Jefferson and Madison's use of the words "commerce" and "trade" was not incidental. They were not writing about American *settlement* on the Mississippi, but American *trade* down the length of the river. At a time when overland travel was lengthy and unreliable, settlers depended on the vast network of rivers that crisscrossed the Midwest and deep South. This latticework of western waterways eventually reached the Mississippi River.

There was more at stake than economic prosperity. If the United States could not guarantee their economy, western settlers might be tempted to form their own nation or build an alliance with the Europeans. Nor was it coincidental that these fears came in the 1780's. The same concerns about the union guided Madison's actions at the Constitutional Convention. Madison feared that the Articles of Confederation did not provide the means for the United States to preserve the union against internal tensions or defend it against foreign threats. Madison specifically worried that the Articles would not guarantee western trade down the Mississippi.[3]

Jefferson and Madison saw Louisiana within their own broad understanding of independence, a concept of particular power in the United States. Once free of the British government, Americans developed a complicated definition that applied to individuals as well as to the United States as a whole. When George Washington warned against "entangling alliances" with other nations, for example, he was not calling for American isolation. He sought a vigorous system of trade and diplomacy between the United States and Europe. But, like Jefferson and Madison, Washington feared what would happen if a foreign power wielded too much influence over the American government.

This subtle distinction between isolation and independence was equally important to individual settlers. Jefferson and Madison believed that their fellow country*men*—they did not apply these principles of independence to women—should enjoy the freedom to make their own decisions. Jefferson's famous celebration of farmers

---

[3] Banning, *The Sacred Fire of Liberty*, 255-8; Lewis, *The American Union and the Problem of Neighborhood;* Onuf and Onuf, *Federal Union, Modern World*, 103-8; Rakove, *Original Meanings*, 43-6; Tucker and Hendrickson, *Empire of Liberty*, 95-100.

had less to do with the daily reality of working a farm than his belief that a man who owned his own land owned his own vote and could participate freely in public affairs. Jefferson believed that independence would enable Americans to work together on equal terms, not isolate themselves from one another. He worried that political disagreements could destroy everything that had cost Americans so dearly during the Revolution, and he recalled how Rome had become "a republic, rent by the most bitter factions and tumults." Jefferson and Madison hoped the states would remain independent but nonetheless unified.[4]

Few people in the early American republic left a better paper trail than Jefferson. The copious documentation of Jefferson's life has provided material for innumerable biographers. Yet his biography deserves some retelling in this book, in large part because Jefferson provides a useful personification of American independence itself. Jefferson was born in 1743 in Albemarle County, Virginia, a region on the fringe of white settlement. When he was thirty-one, his colleagues in Virginia's colonial legislature selected Jefferson to write their most pointed objection to British policy in the American colonies. Jefferson's "Summary View on the Rights of British North America" became a model for other colonial leaders struggling to express their outrage with the British. Two years later he wrote the Declaration of Independence. Jefferson soon returned to Virginia, where he helped write a constitution for the newly independent state before beginning a difficult tenure as governor of Virginia, plagued by both internal political disputes and the humiliation of a British invasion.[5]

Jefferson emerged from the Revolution convinced that independence and unity were fragile creatures that faced domestic as well as foreign threats.[6] After a lengthy sojourn in Paris as U.S. envoy to France, Jefferson returned in 1789 to serve as the nation's first secretary of state. Jefferson's enthusiasm for the government under the new federal Constitution adopted in 1787 soon gave way to frustration with the growing rift that divided George Washington's

---

[4] Jefferson, Notes on the State of Virginia, in Peterson, ed., The Portable Thomas Jefferson, 254.

[5] Conrad, "Putting Rights Talk in Its Place" in Onuf, ed., Jeffersonian Legacies, 225-43; Maier, American Scripture; Malone, Jefferson the Virginian, 128-42.

[6] The leading biographies of Jefferson remain Dumas Malone's five-volume Jefferson and His Time and Peterson, Thomas Jefferson and the New Nation.

administration. As Vice President John Adams and Secretary of the Treasury Alexander Hamilton's power grew, Jefferson found himself excluded from much of the decisionmaking within the cabinet. "The motion of my blood no longer keeps time with the tumult of the world," Jefferson concluded in September 1793. On New Year's Eve he resigned as secretary of state, returning to Monticello, his plantation in the foothills of the Blue Ridge Mountains, to take charge of his faltering finances. Hamilton followed Jefferson into private life two years later, pursuing a legal career in New York.[7]

Despite his "retirement," Jefferson remained a powerful force in American politics. Three years after leaving the cabinet, he challenged John Adams for the presidency. Jefferson came in a close second, and, by constitutional provision, he became vice president. But this proved a difficult arrangement. By June 1797 one observer reported that "Mr. Jefferson...assures me that the president has not opend [sic] his lips to him on politicks [sic] since his appointment." Adams soon found that his vice president was fostering political opposition within the cabinet itself.[8]

Jefferson abandoned Adams and spent his time with his fellow Virginian and longtime friend, James Madison. Madison's own life, like Jefferson's, provides a way to see how Americans understood independence. At first glance James Madison hardly seemed like the type to run a political opposition. He was a short, bookish man who had endured a directionless youth. The son of a successful plantation owner, the young Madison dreaded the thought of spending his life managing a farm.

It was the American Revolution that provided Madison with his calling. Madison was fascinated by models of political philosophy ranging from ancient Greece to Renaissance Italy to seventeenth-century Britain. It soon became evident that his most impressive talent was the ability to convert those seemingly abstract philosophical principles into practical policies. In 1774 the twenty-three-year-old Madison joined the Orange County Committee of

---

[7] Jefferson, Notes of Conversation with George Washington, 7 February 1793, Boyd, XXV: 154-5; Jefferson to Madison, 9 September 1793, Boyd, XXVI: 10; Banning, *The Jeffersonian Persuasion*, 153-60, 170-4; Peterson, *Thomas Jefferson and the New Nation*, 406-7.
[8] John Dawson to Madison, 4 June 1797, *PJM-17*, 13.

Safety, an organization that mobilized Virginia in opposition to British policy. He entered the Continental Congress in 1780, and, during his service at the state and national level, Madison became transfixed by the profound questions that faced the new nation. How would each state organize itself? How would the states work together? Perhaps most importantly, how would the United States preserve the principles of the Revolution? These questions eventually brought Madison to Philadelphia in 1787, where he became the driving force at the Constitutional Convention.[9]

When Madison went to the first Federal Congress in 1789 as a representative from Virginia, his colleagues deferred to him on constitutional matters. Consider the situation when George Washington assumed the presidency. Madison was everywhere. The president turned to Madison for advice on his inaugural address, and Madison actually wrote the House of Representative's reply to Washington's address. He then wrote Washington's response to the House's reply as well as to the reply of the Senate. Hardly a raging ego, Madison's actions in 1789 instead reflected his primary objective: to get the government on the right path by articulating the constitutional role of each branch of government. How better to do that job than to craft the first public statements of both the executive and the legislature?[10]

During the 1790's Madison grew to share Jefferson's frustrations with the administration, and the two men helped form a political opposition initially known as the Democratic-Republicans, but occasionally called simply the Republicans for short, or the Jeffersonian Republicans in honor of their leader. Adams and his allies in turn became known as Federalists. It can be a confusing title, because the advocates of the Constitution in 1787 were also called federalists. Indeed, the Federalists of the 1790's hoped to make people aware of that connection. But not all federalists from earlier times were Federalists in the 1790's, and some of the most ardent supporters of the Constitution became Democratic-Republicans.[11]

---

[9] Banning, *The Sacred Fire of Liberty*, 113-6, 138-40; Ketcham, *James Madison*, 51-87; Rakove, *James Madison and the Creation of the American Republic*, 8-18.
[10] Banning, *The Sacred Fire of Liberty*, 273-5.
[11] Banning, *The Sacred Fire of Liberty*, 334-65.

Madison left Congress in the spring of 1797, just as Jefferson was beginning his unhappy tenure as vice president. While Jefferson felt constrained within the cabinet, Madison worked to build a nationwide political coalition. Through correspondence, newspaper editorials, and finally by running for office, the Jeffersonian Republicans hoped to wrest power from the Federalists.

Jefferson and Madison discovered the strength of that coalition in 1798, when Republican candidates began to win elections for Congress and state legislatures. When the results from the 1800 election began to arrive, it became clear that Americans were voting for a Republican president. But who would be that president? With political coordination still in its infancy, the two leading Republican candidates—Jefferson and Aaron Burr of New York—split the vote. With no candidate—Adams, Jefferson, or Burr—enjoying a clear majority, it was up to the House of Representatives to decide. As the House vote approached, Burr abandoned his alliance with Jefferson and sought the presidency in his own right. "We consider this a declaration of war, on the part of this band," Jefferson wrote of Burr and his allies. "But their conduct appears to have brought over to us the whole body of Federalists."[12]

Indeed, many Federalists despised Burr even more than they despised Jefferson. Chief among them was Alexander Hamilton. One by one the Federalists endorsed the man who had so actively campaigned against them. It was a strange coalition, but it held. On February 17, 1801, the House chose Thomas Jefferson as the third president of the United States. The acrimony of the Adams Administration together with the disputed election of 1800 led Americans to enact the first major adjustment to the Constitution since approving the Bill of Rights. Concluding that rival candidates were unlikely to make amiable colleagues, Americans passed the twelfth amendment in 1804, which mandated separate candidates for president and vice president.

Republicans soon spoke of the election as the "Revolution of

---

[12]Jefferson to Madison, 18 February 1801, *PJM-17*, 467.

Illustrations (left to right): Top: John Trumbull, *John Adams* (1793), National Portrait Gallery, Smithsonian Institution; John Trumbull, *Alexander Hamilton* (1806); Middle: Gilbert Stuart, *George Washington* (c. 1821); Bottom (left to right): Gilbert Stuart, *James Madison* (c. 1821),©Board of Trustees, National Gallery of Art, Washington. Color plates, page 169. Gilbert Stuart, *Thomas Jefferson* (c. 1821). Color plate, page 170.

1800." This phrase did not necessarily refer to a revolutionary change, but rather a government that had come full circle, revolving to its original principles. And yet there was also room for the Federalists to take some pride in their own actions. By leaving office without resistance, Adams and the Federalists in Congress initiated the stable transfer of power in the United States.

The new regime took office in a new capital. The federal government had moved to the District of Columbia at the end of the Adams Administration, and Jefferson moved into the leaky and incomplete President's House on March 19. Among his first official acts was to offer Madison the post of secretary of state. Unofficially, Jefferson was also inviting Madison to serve as his closest advisor. Years of working together had produced a fruitful partnership. Even their different personal styles made them one of the most effective teams in American politics. Where Jefferson wrote on theoretical matters with eloquence and passion, Madison focused his energy on the practical sphere of government. While Jefferson extolled the virtues of a free society during the 1780's, Madison crafted the Constitution that would make such a system work. When Jefferson articulated the danger of the Federalists during the 1790's, Madison created the party organization that brought the Republicans into power. And as Jefferson developed the nation's foreign and domestic agenda in 1801, it was Madison whom he entrusted to implement those policies.[13]

Louisiana might be distant from Washington, D.C., and it was at the time foreign soil, but Jefferson and Madison nonetheless believed restrictions on American trade would eventually destroy the union. For western settlers, whose numbers grew substantially during the 1780's and '90's, trade depended on the ability to send goods down the Mississippi, which functioned as a gateway to broader trading opportunities on both sides of the Atlantic.[14]

Going into the election of 1800, Jefferson and Madison were confident that the United States would be able to preserve its trade

[13] Ketcham, *James Madison;* McCoy, *The Elusive Republic,* 153-64, 206-18; Peterson, *Thomas Jefferson and the New Nation,* 390-3, 614-5; Rakove, *James Madison and the Creation of the American Republic,* 92-3.
[14] Lewis, *The American Union and the Problem of Neighborhood,* 15.

down the Mississippi River. In 1795 the United States had signed a treaty with Spain that specifically guaranteed Americans the right to deposit their goods in New Orleans for transshipment to the Atlantic. No sooner were Jefferson and Madison at work in 1801, however, than they learned that Spain had returned Louisiana to France. They joined other Americans who responded to the retrocession—as the act became known—with a combination of outrage and indignation. The Treaty of San Ildefonso, which implemented the retrocession, dictated that France would *own* Louisiana, but Spain would continue to *govern* the colony. Rufus King, the American minister to Great Britain, captured the feeling of many Americans when he wrote, "this cesion is intended to have, and may actually produce, Effects injurious to the Union and consequent happiness of the People of the United States."[15]

What were those dangers? That King did not state them indicates that Americans took for granted the consensus they shared. Americans worried that the transfer might nullify the 1795 treaty. Worse still, it might bring international conflicts dangerously close to the United States. Revolutionary France had gone to war with Great Britain in 1793, and the war rapidly expanded to include most of Europe. Americans feared French ambitions in the Americas that might place a powerful, unpredictable, and potentially dangerous regime in control of the Mississippi. Even if the French were benign in their control of Louisiana, Jefferson and Madison worried that the war between France and Britain could easily spread to North America.

The worst news came from New Orleans itself. In November 1802, the Spanish closed New Orleans to all American commerce. Congressmen and Senators decried the Spanish actions, speaking of a "Mississippi Crisis" that threatened the union itself. The Kentucky state legislature passed a resolution condemning the Spanish action. These reactions proved that western settlers shared the administration's sentiments. But this rising anger throughout the western frontiers of the United States did not reassure Jefferson and his advisors. They worried that the Mississippi Crisis might precipitate

---

[15] Rufus King to Madison, 29 March 1801, *PJM-SS1*, 55. See also Claiborne to Madison, 3 January 1803, *PJM-SS4*, 237; Onuf and Onuf, *Federal Union, Modern World*, 151-3.

tensions that could undo the fragile union. Whether Kentuckians were serious about disunion remains open for debate. They did not take any concrete steps toward creating a separate government, but people in Washington became convinced that western settlers would indeed leave the union unless the federal government restored American trading privileges in New Orleans. Both foreign intervention and domestic unrest threatened to obliterate an independent and unified nation. In 1784, Madison had feared an "impolitic & perverse" Spanish policy. Now the Mississippi Crisis had turned his worst fears into a reality which he believed could lead to disunion.[16]

Americans were uncertain whether closing New Orleans constituted an aggressive act by the Spanish government, an insidious plan by France and Spain, or simply the act of a rogue intendant.[17] Madison preferred to believe the latter, for it created the possibility of a speedy reconciliation. He contacted Carlos Martinez de Yrujo, the Spanish minister to the United States, demanding that the Spanish government rein in its colonial officials. "It is impossible to see in ...these measures, any thing less than a direct and gross violation of the terms as well as the spirit of the Treaty of 1795," Madison wrote. Madison considered this a personal betrayal because the two men were close acquaintances. Yrujo's wife, an American, was a close friend of James and Dolly Madison. Madison's measured tones in his letter to Yrujo reflected Madison's reserved nature as well as the courtesies common to diplomatic correspondence.[18] As the weeks dragged by and the Spanish showed no inclination to change, Madison concluded that it was "not likely that Spain will be more flexible than she is at present."[19]

In addition to Spanish recalcitrance, Americans worried about French adventurism. Reports from Europe indicated that France intended to eject the Spanish caretakers from Louisiana, replacing them with a massive contingent of French troops. Jefferson concluded that "the session of Louisiana and the Floridas by Spain to France works more sorely on the U.S. The day that France takes possession of

---

[16] Lewis, "Jefferson's Mississippi Crisis and the Problem of Union, 1801-1803."

[17] Madison to William Hulings, 29 November 1802, *PJM-SS4*, 153-4; Madison to Meeker, 10 December 1802, *PJM-SS4*, 185; Madison to Jefferson, 21 December 1802, *PJM-SS4*, 210; Madison to King, 23 December 1802, *PJM-SS4*, 216-7.

[18] Madison to Carlos Martinez de Yrujo, 25 November 1802, *PJM-SS4*, 140.

[19] Madison to Charles Pinckney, 25 October 1802, *PJM-SS4*, 55.

N. Orleans fixes the sentence which is to restrain her forever within her low water mark."[20] Jefferson even considered seeking a declaration of war or establishing an alliance with Great Britain if France attempted to implement the retrocession. He soon dismissed both plans, however, realizing instead that there was little the United States could do.[21] Confiding to Pierre Samuel du Pont de Nemours—whose family was already amassing a fortune from gunpowder mills in Delaware, a fortune the Duponts diversified later in the century—Jefferson described "the inevitable consequences of their [the French] taking possession of Louisiana." Jefferson predicted disaster for the United States and war between the United States and France or France and Great Britain. In contrast, Jefferson believed a resolution of the Mississippi crisis would preserve American independence and unity while keeping the United States clear of any alliances that might drag it into European conflicts.[22]

Still, neither Jefferson's zeal to control the Mississippi nor his planning revealed any desire to acquire *all* of Louisiana. Only in characteristic but occasional flights of fancy did Jefferson write about an American empire that stretched to the Pacific. Such comments were few and far between. They appeared in occasional letters discussing Jefferson's *ideal* model for the future. His detailed reports to friends and confidants indicate a more pragmatic mindset that guided him during the crisis of 1802. His struggle was to respond to the retrocession in a way that would preserve rather than expand the existing union. As Jefferson and Madison soon learned, the greatest problem they faced was a European community that often ignored American concerns.

In planning with his closest advisors, Jefferson developed modest goals. He wanted to establish American sovereignty over the mouth of the Mississippi River, specifically New Orleans and West Florida—the area of the Gulf Coast due east of New Orleans. This would guarantee the prosperity of American settlers *east* of the Mississippi rather than create a new home for Americans *west* of the Mississippi. He was thinking of settlers in places like Ohio, Kentucky,

---

[20] Jefferson to Livingston, 18 April 1802, Ford, VIII: 143.

[21] Jefferson to Livingston, 18 April 1802, Ford, VIII: 143.

[22] Jefferson to Pierre Samuel du Pont de Nemours, 25 April 1802, in Malone, ed., *Correspondence between Thomas Jefferson and Pierre Samuel du Pont de Nemours*, 47.

and Tennessee, who depended on free navigation of the Mississippi for their livelihood. Jefferson had sought this goal for years, but the retrocession created problems that made American sovereignty over New Orleans all the more vital.[23]

---

[23] Jefferson to Livingston, 18 April 1802, Ford: IX, 363-9. See also Jefferson to John Breckenridge, 12 August 1803, *Jefferson Papers*, Reel 46.

CHAPTER THREE

"THE PROSPECT OF ACCOMMODATION"

Robert R. Livingston, the American minister to Paris, felt isolated and frustrated. He felt ignored by his distant countrymen and ignored by the Europeans who surrounded him. Like Jefferson and Madison, and, for that matter, like the residents of Louisiana, Livingston had been stunned by news of the retrocession of Louisiana. Like them, he recoiled at the new Spanish restrictions on American merchants. But, unlike his countrymen, it was not that France and Spain had both acted against the United States that infuriated Livingston. It was the fact that no one had discussed the matter with him.

Robert R. Livingston was something of an anomaly within the Republican leadership. Most of Jefferson's appointees were southerners like himself or allies with a long history of loyalty to the Jeffersonian cause. Livingston was neither. A native New Yorker, Livingston was the third of eleven children and the oldest son of one of the richest men in the nation. His family abounded with politicians. Livingston's father had been a prominent figure in the politics of colonial New York. His younger brother, Edward, had served as a Congressman in the 1790's before becoming both mayor of New York City, an office appointed by the governor, and U.S. district attorney for New York, an office appointed by the president.

It was in the tumult of revolution that Livingston first worked with Jefferson. Livingston served in the Second Continental Congress, and in June 1776 he joined Jefferson, John Adams, Benjamin Franklin, and Roger Sherman on the committee that drafted the Declaration of Independence. Although he was the acknowledged leader of the New York delegation to the Continental Congress, a position of tremendous influence given New York's financial and political power, Livingston proved to be a passive member of the committee of five that drafted the Declaration. But his presence on the committee established his relationship with Jefferson, both men playing roles in the nation's affairs, but with the Virginian overshadowing the New Yorker.[1]

Livingston and Jefferson's lives continued on parallel tracks. Like Jefferson, Livingston soon left Philadelphia for his home state where, also like Jefferson, he helped write his state's constitution. Livingston's introduction to diplomacy came in 1781, when he began a two-year tenure as secretary of foreign affairs, precursor to the office of secretary of state that Jefferson held less than a decade later. As much as anyone, Livingston appreciated the limitations of the Articles of Confederation, which undermined his diplomatic efforts. With the national government possessing only limited powers, any agreement between the "United States" and a foreign power faced the imminent likelihood of challenges by any one of the state governments. Besides, the general government's limited funds provided Livingston with few diplomatic or military resources to realize American goals. Despite their shared desire for constitutional reforms, Jefferson and Livingston went their separate ways during the 1780's. Livingston became a disgruntled member of the Constitutional Convention and he opposed ratification. Both Livingston and Jefferson advocated national policies that would help their home states, and these regional differences brought them into conflict.[2]

During the 1790's, Livingston joined forces with Jefferson and Madison, helping establish Republican strength in New York at a time when the Federalist Alexander Hamilton dominated the state's politics. The entire Livingston family migrated to the Jeffersonians. Edward Livingston, at that time a Congressman, abandoned his initial support for Aaron Burr and voted for Jefferson in the contested 1801 House of Representatives' vote that determined the presidency. Jefferson repaid both Livingstons. He selected Edward for the district attorney's office in New York. He offered Robert the post of secretary

[1] Dangerfield, *Chancellor Robert R. Livingston*, 78-80.
[2] Dangerfield, *Chancellor Robert R. Livingston*, 211-2, 16-50; Rakove, *Original Meanings*, 11.

of the navy. When Robert declined, Jefferson offered him the appointment to France.[3]

There was more to the appointment than mere patronage, for Livingston was a logical choice. He shared Jefferson and Madison's attitudes toward France. All three men were Francophiles who nonetheless recoiled at the excesses of the revolutionary regime. Like many other Americans, Livingston had financial interests in France, and he believed that a settlement of the Louisiana question would help resolve his private concerns as well as fulfill his public responsibilities. In a modern context, this might easily appear a conflict of interest. But public affairs operated by different standards in the early nineteenth century, and Livingston's personal interests made him all the more likely to promote amicable relations. The same rules had applied to Jefferson during his own tenure in Paris, when he attempted to settle both personal and national debts.

Yet for all his strengths, Livingston possessed serious limitations. He spoke almost no French, a problem made all the worse by the fact that he was partially deaf. As tensions between the United States and France grew in the wake of the retrocession of Louisiana, problems in communication between diplomats of the two nations were quite real.[4]

Livingston possessed no illusions about the task before him. As American diplomats learned throughout the late eighteenth and early nineteenth centuries, European officials had little time—or interest—to invest in American affairs. Livingston dispatched numerous reports to Washington complaining that the French were dragging their feet. Livingston pleaded with the French to pressure Spain to respect the provisions of the Treaty of San Lorenzo—the 1795 treaty with the United States which guaranteed that Spain would never resell Louisiana—only to report that the French "spoke of the treaty as waste paper."[5]

The experience was galling for Livingston, and Jefferson was equally irritated when he learned of the French behavior. It was

---

[3] Dangerfield, *Chancellor Robert R. Livingston*, 301-5.
[4] Dangerfield, *Chancellor Robert R. Livingston*, 183.
[5] Livingston to Madison, 10 November 1802, *PJM-SS4*, 110; Livingston to Madison, 11 November 1802, *PJM-SS4*, 115. See also Livingston to Madison, 20 December 1802, *PJM-SS4*, 204.

"THE PROSPECT OF ACCOMMODATION"

impossible for Jefferson and Livingston not to interpret the situation in personal terms. Both men were members of the American aristocracy and were accustomed to deference and respect. Thousands of New York settlers bowed to the Livingstons, not just because the Livingstons were wealthy but also because so many of those settlers lived on lands that the Livingstons chose to rent rather than to sell. With over 200 slaves following his every command, Jefferson had become familiar with power long before he became president. Jefferson and Livingston believed that their experiences during the Revolution mirrored the experience of the entire nation, and they interpreted the personal insults of the French governments as insults to the United States. Jefferson had encountered similar treatment during his tenure as American minister to France in the 1780s. Livingston's reception only confirmed Jefferson's opinion that Europe was corrupt and governed by despots who refused to treat the United States as a legitimate partner in world affairs.

As long as the French intended to establish control over Louisiana, they had no reason to accede to American demands. So Livingston's diplomatic initiatives stalled. It soon became clear to the Americans that there was little chance of preventing the French from implementing the retrocession. As Livingston informed Madison in September 1802, "the French Government had determined to take possession [of Louisiana]... so that you must consider the business as absolutely determined on."[6] He later reported an incident in which he "had reason to think that [the French] began to waver but we had nothing to offer but money & commercial advantages." In the absence of greater influence with the French, Livingston doubted any change in the situation would occur.[7]

Nor did any more promising news come from Spain. Charles Pinckney, the American envoy to Madrid, wrote about the Spanish reaction with a degree of anger and sarcasm that resonated with his superiors in Washington. He complained to Madison of the Spanish minister's "manner of expressing himself on the subject of the navigation of the Mississippi" and wrote that the Spanish believed the

[6] Livingston to Madison, 1 September 1802, *PJM-SS3*, 536.
[7] Livingston to Madison, 11 April 1803, *PJM-SS4*, 500.

United States had no right to make demands for *"the Favour* as he calls it of our being allowed a Deposit at New Orleans...Spaniards themselves considered that & all our other rights as mere favours springing from the Generosity of the King."[8]

As these reports reached Washington in 1802 and 1803, they confirmed Jefferson and Madison's belief that no other nation should control the Mississippi River. They determined to acquire New Orleans and West Florida before the French established themselves in Louisiana. This mantra increasingly consumed the president's attention. In January 1803, Madison wrote a coded letter that ordered Livingston to offer France up to $2 million for the land, an unprecedented amount of money in a nation that was still shouldering massive debts from the American Revolution. "If less will not do we are prepared to meet it," Madison wrote, "but it is hoped that less will do and that the prospect of accommodation will concur with other motives in postponing the [French] expedition to louisiana."[9]

All of these developments left Jefferson and his advisors increasingly frustrated with the situation in Paris. Much as he might blame French ministers, Jefferson also had reason to doubt his own diplomat. "I hope the game mr. Livingston says he is playing is a candid & honourable one," Jefferson worried.[10] The President decided to bolster Livingston's efforts by dispatching a second diplomat to France. In January 1803 Jefferson summoned his friend and protégé, James Monroe.

Jefferson's friendship with Monroe was fundamentally different from his relationships with Madison or Livingston. Madison and Livingston were the president's contemporaries in both age and experience. Each man could in his own right lay claim to membership in the small cadre that had helped found the nation. Monroe was of a different generation. Where Jefferson, Madison, and Livingston were poised to begin public careers during the Revolution, Monroe was only eighteen years old in 1776, a student in his second year at the College of William and Mary. Before the end of the term, and before

---

[8] Charles Pinckney to James Madison, 4 May 1803, *PJM-SS4*, 571. See also John Graham to Madison, 7 May 1803.
[9] Madison to Livingston, 18 January 1803, *PJM-SS4*, 260. See also Livingston to Madison, 18 February 1803, *ASP: Foreign Relations*: II: 533-4.
[10] Jefferson to Madison, 19 March 1803, *PJM-SS4*, 434.

"THE PROSPECT OF ACCOMMODATION"

the United States declared independence, Monroe abandoned William and Mary for a commission in the Virginia Infantry. Like most states, Virginia maintained its own military force, which often operated in conjunction with, but was never under the authority of, George Washington's Continental Army. Monroe eventually did serve in the Continental Army, but by 1780 he was back in Virginia, where he provided intelligence on the British army for Virginia's governor, Thomas Jefferson. It was only the first in a string of assignments where Monroe served as Jefferson's emissary.[11]

A man without sons, Jefferson cultivated the talents of numerous young men from Virginia, hoping to guide the state's next generation of leaders. Nobody proved to be a more eager apprentice than James Monroe. Monroe left the military and moved to the new capital at Richmond where Jefferson personally instructed him in the law. In the years that followed, Jefferson also became Monroe's political advocate. Jefferson helped Monroe win election to the Virginia General Assembly and the United States Senate. Monroe served as American minister to France from 1794 to 1796, a post Jefferson held a decade before, and won election as governor of Virginia in 1799, the office Jefferson held during the Revolution.

By 1803, Monroe was still in the governor's office, at forty-four a seasoned politician and an experienced diplomat. In fact, Monroe barely knew a period in his adult life when he was *not* in government. Much as Americans like Monroe endorsed rotation in office and limited terms, they usually meant rotating from one office to another rather than leaving government altogether. While Monroe planned to take a hiatus from public office after his term as governor expired, he was less averse to politics than he was interested in improving his finances. Like so many of his contemporaries, Monroe's expenses as a public official often exceeded his public salary. He hoped to build a legal practice and settle his growing personal debt. As Monroe himself later put it, referring to himself in the third person, "he resumed his station at the bar with attention to devote himself to the profession

---

[11] Ammon, *James Monroe*, 7-32.

until he should place his affairs in an independent state." [12]

Unlike Madison and Jefferson, who displayed so much public reserve, Monroe was an opinionated, obstinate, and remarkably thin-skinned man. The word that most often comes to mind when considering James Monroe is "combative." This term had a literal meaning during the American Revolution, when Monroe led frontal assaults on the British, eventually suffering severe wounds at the Battle of Trenton in 1776. That passion was still in place almost twenty years later. In 1797, the conflict between the Federalists and Republicans almost led to a dual between Monroe and Alexander Hamilton.[13] Monroe's vitality seemed all the more striking in contrast to an aging and ailing Livingston. Jefferson predicted that the same fervor Monroe brought to domestic politics would enable Monroe to break the diplomatic stalemate in Paris.[14]

Monroe's departure presented Jefferson and Madison with a final opportunity to influence the negotiations. It was in this context that Madison composed his March 2, 1803, instructions, the lengthy dispatch in which the secretary of state laid out the administration's goals in Paris. The instructions encapsulated all that men like Jefferson and Madison had come to believe about the Mississippi River, the American union, and the situation in Europe. Foreign control over commerce down the river posed a dire threat to domestic harmony, since irate western settlers might seek disunion. Foreign possession of the Gulf Coast constituted a threat to national security, since it gave foreign powers easy access to the nation's borders. Jefferson and Madison decided, "the object in view is to procure by just and satisfactory arrangements, a Cession to the United States, of New Orleans, and of West and East Florida."

Monroe carried Madison's instructions with him on a quick Atlantic passage. He reached France exactly one month after his

---

[12] Brown, ed., *The Autobiography of James Monroe*, 153; Ammon, *James Monroe*, 203.
[13] Freeman, "Dueling as Politics," 298-9; Jan Lewis, "'The Blessings of Domestic Society': Thomas Jefferson's Family and the Transformation of American Politics," in Onuf, ed., *Jeffersonian Legacies*, 119-22.
[14] Ammon, *James Monroe*, 204-7.

March 8 departure. Four days later he was in Paris. Confident in his abilities and dedicated to fulfilling Jefferson's orders, Monroe prepared to rejuvenate American negotiations. He was well aware of the problems Livingston had encountered during his tenure as American minister. He had no way of knowing what the French had in store.

Chapter Four
OPPORTUNITY

In both Louisiana and the United States, the reaction to the retrocession was just that: a reaction. Jefferson and Madison were wise to send a special envoy, but they were deluding themselves if they believed that American policy alone would determine the outcome of the Mississippi Crisis. From a European perspective, the United States was a weak nation very much on the periphery of world affairs. If the United States could be an ally, so much the better, but no European leader would bank his future on relations with the United States.

The reason the United States faced a Mississippi Crisis had its roots in Europe. As a result, the solution would have to come from Europe. Understanding why the United States found itself negotiating with France for the acquisition of Louisiana—and how those negotiations eventually ended—requires a dramatic geographic shift away from the New World to the titanic struggle to determine the fate of the Old.

Warfare had been a periodic reality in Europe throughout the eighteenth century. These conflicts often spread to the Americas. The contest of empires precipitated the cession of Louisiana in 1763, and European tensions elevated the American Revolution from a struggle within the British Empire into a war on a global scale. In 1793 the French Revolution sparked a European war, and, while the major combatants signed a peace treaty in 1801, they remained suspicious of one another. By 1803, when Monroe left the United States, many people in Europe and the Americas assumed war would soon resume.

Monroe certainly appreciated this state of affairs. As he crossed the Atlantic, the special envoy knew he would be confronting the most imposing figure in world affairs, a man eleven years his junior who nonetheless had mastered the politics of his own country while challenging the armed forces of his neighbors. Securing a resolution to the Mississippi Crisis would mean satisfying the wishes of Napoleon Bonaparte.

People have seen Napoleon Bonaparte through a variety of lenses because he was at once a general and a head of state, a revolutionary and a dictator. One of the best ways to understand Napoleon, at least in the context of the Louisiana Purchase, is to see him in comparison to Jefferson, Madison, and Monroe. Like those three Americans, Napoleon was the product of revolution, but it was a fundamentally different revolution from the one that created the United States, and Napoleon entered that revolution with a background that could not have been more different from that of the three Virginians. He lacked both the wealth and political connections that enabled the three Virginians to secure high office. Rather than the son of the Virginia gentry, Napoleon was the child of a struggling Corsican family. His early career also followed a different trajectory. Jefferson and Madison emerged as political leaders first, and Monroe's military service was brief before he, too, began a political career. Napoleon remained first and foremost a soldier. A general at age twenty-four, he was the leading military figure in France by age twenty-seven. He then entered the political arena, first joining the ruling elite and then subduing it. In 1799, the thirty-year-old Bonaparte became First Consul, the undisputed leader of France. Three years later he reigned supreme, confirming his power with an overwhelming vote in a national referendum that asked a single question: "Shall Napoleon Bonaparte be consul for life?"

Robert Livingston had no doubts of Napoleon's power. "The first Consul acts entirely for himself," he informed Madison in July 1802. "[N]o one about him has any personal consequence or consideration. Nothing is proposed but by himself, his will is never opposed & if any

Jacques-Louis David, *Napoleon in His Study* (1812), © Board of Trustees, National Gallery of Art, Washington. Color plate, page 171.

consultations are held they only extend to details relative to matters already resolved." Livingston added a passage that confirmed the administration's worst fears. "It will be proper for you to know that this is no longer *a republic*...That this is the government of *one man whose will is the law.*"[1]

As Napoleon consolidated his control over France, he began to dream of a rejuvenated empire overseas. He was not alone. Other Frenchmen had long regretted their government's decision to surrender Louisiana. The French had practical reasons for wanting Louisiana. A powerful French presence in North America would force the British to reinforce garrisons in Canada, which in turn would reduce British military power in Europe. Perhaps most important, however, Louisiana would contribute to Napoleon's political economy. The massive plantations dotting the landscape of France's Caribbean colonies produced tremendous profits, but they depended on outside sources for the most basic necessities. Louisiana had proven unprofitable for both the French and the Spanish, but Napoleon believed it could provide exactly the basic necessities that would sustain his Caribbean empire.[2]

It was for these reasons that Napoleon orchestrated the retrocession in 1800, the act that caused so much fear in Washington and propelled the agenda of the Jefferson Administration. Napoleon soon decided to eject the Spanish caretakers and assume direct control, but the Spanish dug in their heels. By 1802 Napoleon was so frustrated with the Spanish government that he warned "if they continue this system [of delay], it will end with a thunderbolt."[3]

Enter Robert Livingston, who responded to the retrocession without ever really grasping Napoleon's anger toward Spain. Although he knew that France and Spain were at odds over Louisiana, Livingston—like other members of the Jefferson Administration—tended to see both countries at part of the same problem. American policymakers concluded that their erratic behavior in the Mississippi Valley made France and Spain equally dangerous to the United States.

---

[1] Livingston to Madison, 20 May 1802, *PJM-SS3*, 231-2.
[2] DeConde, *This Affair of Louisiana*, 75-81, 99-105; Tucker and Hendrickson, *Empire of Liberty*, 102-5.
[3] Napoleon Bonaparte to Gouvion St. Cyr, Quoted in DeConde, *This Affair of Louisiana*, 104.

But the Americans also tended to overestimate French security. Napoleon faced numerous challenges, from the Spanish and Great Britain. In addition, the French Empire had internal problems of its own.

Napoleon's plan to establish French power in the Americas faced its greatest threat in the Caribbean colony of Saint-Domingue. Located on the western half of the island of Hispaniola, Saint-Domingue bordered the Spanish colony of Dominica. Christopher Columbus' first steps in the New World had been on the sandy beaches of Hispaniola. Since then, France and Spain had built a system of plantations that covered the island, and it was these plantations that Napoleon hoped to supply from Louisiana.

Like much of the Caribbean, the vast majority of Saint-Domingue's population was of African descent, mostly enslaved. But it was the free people of color who first began to mobilize in Saint-Domingue. In 1791, free people of color argued that the principles of the French Revolution should apply to them, that they should be treated as citizens equal to whites. When white settlers refused to surrender their privileges to their free non-white neighbors, Saint-Domingue descended into civil war. [4]

Initially, few free people of color sought an abolition of slavery. Indeed, many of them owned slaves themselves. However, when whites refused to implement equality for all free people, Saint-Domingue's free people of color began to form alliances with slaves. This was not an independence movement like that of the United States, nor did Americans endorse the struggle for equality in the Caribbean. The struggle in Saint-Domingue was an internal revolution, and France was the model for the Caribbean revolutionaries. As Toussaint-Louverture, a free man of color and nominal leader of the revolutionary movement, stated, "[Do not] forget that I represent France and that the Revolution shall always continue to be a bond for us with the mother country."[5]

---

[4] Langley, *The Americas in the Age of Revolution*, 107-17.
[5] Quoted in Langley, *The Americas in the Age of Revolution*, 123.

Napoleon ignored Toussaint's statements of loyalty and decided to restore white authority by force. In 1802 an armada with over 30,000 seasoned troops left France for the Caribbean. Their commander, General Charles Leclerc, was Napoleon's brother-in-law. Leclerc predicted a brief excursion to suppress an uprising of untrained, uneducated slaves. He was sorely disappointed. Napoleon's soldiers fell victim to the revolutionaries, and to disease. By the end of 1802 the French campaign to control Saint-Domingue became a disaster that dwarfed any French defeat in Europe. Leclerc himself was among the victims, dying of yellow fever. Less than a year after it sailed, the French army collapsed.

Many white Americans expressed ambivalence toward events in Saint-Domingue. Most Republicans were eager to see Toussaint's regime end, nobody more so than Thomas Jefferson. Men like Jefferson and Madison were deathly afraid of the revolution in Saint-Domingue because they worried it would provide a model for American slaves. Jefferson condemned the revolutionaries as "cannibals of the terrible republic."[6] And yet Americans also grasped the way that revolt in Saint-Domingue might affect French planning in Louisiana. Rufus King wrote in 1802, "the establishment of this Colony [Louisiana] is a darling object and will be pursued with ardor...unless the affairs of Saint-Domingo shall for the moment derange the plan."[7]

King was correct. News of the Caribbean debacle left Napoleon badly shaken. He was preparing to renounce his peace with Great Britain and renew the European war. For this, he needed to focus his men, resources, and finances on Europe. Napoleon could not afford the cost in men and money of sinking into the quagmire of Saint-Domingue. During the winter of 1802-1803, Napoleon reached two decisions. First, he made plans to abandon Saint-Domingue. Second, he reconsidered the retrocession of Louisiana he had championed just two years earlier. He had sought Louisiana to buttress the commerce and the defense of France's lucrative colonies in the Caribbean, and

[6] Jefferson to Aaron Burr, 11 February 1799, quoted in Mathewson, "Jefferson and Haiti," 217.
[7] Rufus King to Madison, 5 March 1802, PJM-SS3, 3-4. See also Matthewson, "Jefferson and Haiti," 209-19; Onuf, "'To Declare Them a Free and Independent People,'" 1-46.

now Louisiana served little purpose without Saint-Domingue. As the Spanish had done in 1800, Napoleon dispensed with Louisiana.

Unfortunately, he had no customers in Europe. He was at odds with Spain because he had made clear his intention of removing the Spanish from Louisiana. And he was in no position to negotiate with his primary antagonist, the British. That left few prospects in Europe. No other European power expressed imperial ambitions in North America substantial enough to make them gamble on Louisiana.[8]

The first indication of Napoleon's solution came in April 1803 when he summoned his minister of the public treasury, Francois Barbé-Marbois. Napoleon informed Barbé-Marbois that "I think of ceding it [Louisiana] to the United States...I already consider the Colony as completely lost, and it seems to me that in the hands of that growing power it will be more useful to the policy, and even to the commerce of France than if I should try to keep it."[9] Unknown to Napoleon, Madison had reached an identical conclusion only a month earlier. In his instructions to Livingston and Monroe, Madison predicted that "the instability of the peace of Europe, the attitude taken by Great Britain, the languishing state of the French finances, and the absolute necessity of either abandoning the West India Islands or of sending thither large armaments at great expence all contribute at the present crisis to prepare in the French Government a disposition to listen to an arrangement."[10] But even Madison did not predict the scope of Napoleon's plan. "It is not only New Orleans that I cede," Napoleon announced. "It is the whole colony, without reserve...to attempt obstinately to retain it is folly."[11]

Napoleon had reached his decision at the very moment that Jefferson, Madison, and Livingston were complaining about French intransigence. It was a radical shift in French foreign policy.

Napoleon's choice of representatives was telling. Normally he would assign his foreign minister, Charles Maurice de Talleyrand-Périgord, to handle the negotiations. Instead, Napoleon chose Francois

---

[8] DeConde, *This Affair of Louisiana*, 147-75.
[9] Lyon, *The Man Who Sold Louisiana*, 118-9.
[10] Madison to Livingston and Monroe, 2 March 1803, *PJM-SS4*, 365-6.
[11] Adams, *History of the United States*, II: 27.

Barbé-Marbois, his minister of the treasury. Barbé-Marbois was an expert on the Americans. This was no small matter in 1803 when few Frenchmen had any diplomatic dealings with the young republic that they considered strange, distant, and culturally unsophisticated. From 1779 to 1785, Barbé-Marbois served a variety of diplomatic posts in the newly independent United States. During his tenure in Philadelphia Barbé-Marbois met and married Elizabeth Moore, the daughter of an influential Pennsylvania politician. Barbé-Marbois had contacts throughout the United States, and seemed well-positioned to quickly discern American goals in the negotiations.[12]

All of these changes in France remained unknown to the American leadership. Although some Americans like Madison had surmised that the collapse of Napoleon's Caribbean empire might give the United States some leverage in the negotiations for Louisiana, they did now know how far Napoleon had proceeded in his plans to dispense with Louisiana. As he contemplated the situation in Saint-Domingue, Napoleon decided an agreement with the United States might enable him to settle affairs on both sides of the Atlantic. It was time to summon the Americans.

---

[12] Lyon, *The Man Who Sold Louisiana*, 18.

CHAPTER FIVE

"THE CREDIT AND CHARACTER OF OUR NATION"

Napoleon issued his orders to Barbé-Marbois on April 11. Monroe reached Paris the following day. Although he had ignored Robert Livingston for almost two years, Napoleon and his advisors possessed a keen understanding of American diplomatic goals. They certainly knew that the Americans were eager to purchase Louisiana. The arrival of a second diplomat only made the American intentions more clear. In yet another example of serendipity, Barbé-Marbois and Monroe shared a long acquaintance. The association began in the United States in 1789, when the Frenchman was a diplomat in the United States, and Monroe was serving in Congress. The contact continued in Europe, when Monroe served as American minister to France.[1]

The timing simply could not have been better. Not only did Napoleon and Madison reach similar conclusions at the same time about the importance of Saint-Domingue, but the means Napoleon devised to solve the dilemma arrived as if on queue. There could not have been a better set of conditions for Napoleon to sell Louisiana to the United States. The close proximity of Napoleon's change of heart and Monroe's arrival can create the false belief that Jefferson and Madison's decisions were driving Louisiana's fate. But it was the action of slaves and free people of color in Saint-Domingue who shaped Napoleon's Louisiana.

This does not mean that Americans were irrelevant. In fact, the peaceful transfer of power from the Federalists and Republicans after the election of 1800 had considerable impact. When Napoleon decided to dispense with Louisiana in 1803, he had every reason to believe

---

[1] Ammon, *James Monroe*, 139-40; Lyon, *The Man Who Sold Louisiana*, 46, 86, 91.

that the United States was a stable regime that would honor its agreements.

Americans dismissed the first indications of a change in French policy. On the same day that Napoleon ordered Barbé-Marbois to cede Louisiana to the United States, his foreign minister, de Talleyrand, floated an idea past Livingston: if France wanted to sell Louisiana, would the United States be interested? Livingston was more stunned than relieved. His response provided a powerful restatement of American goals. "I told him no," Livingston later recalled. "that our wishes extended only to New Orleans & the Floridas." Over the next day, Livingston scrambled for de Talleyrand to repeat this offer, but nothing was forthcoming. He eventually concluded that de Talleyrand meant to tease the Americans, and his comments did not constitute a legitimate offer. By the time Monroe spent his first full day in Paris, April 13, Livingston had apparently decided that the offer was merely a ruse to judge American intentions.[2]

The American delegation in Paris was distracted by its own problems. Monroe doubted Livingston's diplomatic talents. Livingston took offense at Monroe's presence, which he interpreted as an insult on the part of an administration too eager to reward Virginians. He complained to Madison that "it is important that I Should be thought to Stand as well with our Government as any other person. If So, my age & the Stations I have held entitled me not to have any person placed above me in the line I fill."[3] The two Americans would have to negotiate a truce between each other before they could engage the French. Monroe sent an olive branch on April 13, when he invited Livingston to join him for dinner with two other Americans. It proved to be an uncomfortable gathering, with the disgruntled diplomats occupying center stage.

Did they notice Barbé-Marbois when he saw Monroe and Livingston? Or did it come as a surprise when Barbé-Marbois interrupted the meal and asked Livingston to step aside for a private conversation? Monroe and Livingston left no record of their reaction.

---

[2] Livingston to Madison, 11 April 1803, *PJM-SS4*, 500; Dangerfield, *Chancellor Robert R. Livingston*, 360.
[3] Livingston to Madison, 17 April 1803, *PJM-SS4*, 525.

Whether it was mere coincidence or whether Barbé-Marbois searched for the Americans in order to expedite Napoleon's orders also remains a mystery. The Americans had no indication of what Barbé-Marbois had to offer, preferring instead to ask the Frenchmen to wait until they had completed their meal. Later that evening, while the Americans drank coffee, Barbé-Marbois returned. Monroe watched as Barbé-Marbois presented Napoleon's proposition: the immediate sale of Louisiana. He invited Livingston to a meeting later that evening in which they would discuss the details.[4]

Livingston accepted the offer without hesitation. At the last possible moment—when Monroe was present in Paris but had not formally presented his credentials—Livingston believed he might yet settle the crisis, in the process redeeming the trust and reputation he considered damaged by Monroe's appointment. Livingston and Barbé-Marbois talked late into the night of April 13. They began to speak of a territorial cession from France to the United States. But exactly what form would their cession take? Livingston was still thinking in terms of the Jefferson Administration's goal: New Orleans and the Gulf Coast for 30 million francs. Barbé-Marbois soon presented very different terms: the sale of both Upper and Lower Louisiana for 100 million francs. The extent of Napoleon's offer came as a shock to the Americans. He was presenting a bill of goods the Americans had not even requested. Thrown off balance, Livingston and Monroe struggled to catch up with Napoleon's plan to execute a land sale of unprecedented size.[5]

Monroe was not altogether pleased with this turn of events. "I hesitated on the idea of his going alone," he later informed Madison. He considered Livingston's decision to rush into negotiations foolhardy, and "intimated delicately that too much zeal might do harm, that a little reserve might have a better effect." After all, Livingston and Monroe had not even conducted a thorough discussion of Jefferson and Madison's instructions. Needless to say, the "little reserve" that Monroe advocated would mean postponing

---

[4] Ammon, *James Monroe*, 210-1; Dangerfield, *Chancellor Robert R. Livingston*, 363.
[5] Ammon, *James Monroe*, 210-1; Dangerfield, *Chancellor Robert R. Livingston*, 363.

negotiations until Monroe could join them. Livingston ignored Monroe's concerns, accepted the offer in principle, and began negotiating the details with Barbé-Marbois.[6]

This was as much a story of ego as it was one of national priorities. Throughout his life, Monroe had exploded in situations when he believed his honor was under attack or had been denied the opportunities to which he was entitled. Nor was Livingston driven entirely by a diplomatic agenda. He, too, had an ego to defend against the offense he perceived from the administration's decision to dispatch Monroe. Settling the matter without the "little reserve" that Monroe so desperately sought would enable Livingston to take all the credit, while punishing the upstart Monroe who seemed so eager to take charge of the negotiations.

Despite the emerging feud between Monroe and Livingston, both men nonetheless agreed in general terms. As Monroe later recalled, the American diplomats "ascertained...that the First Consul would cede no part of the province if he did not cede it all." Given these circumstances, they "did not hesitate between the alternatives."[7] Livingston and Monroe had few qualms about exceeding their mandate and accepting the French offer to sell all of Louisiana. At the same time, they remained committed to the central goals of establishing American security in the Southwest and American control over the Mississippi River. Of critical importance to the Americans were guarantees the Louisiana they purchased included New Orleans and the Floridas. Here, too, they shared the same response, this time one of disappointment as Barbé-Marbois was forced to acknowledge that any French claim to the Floridas was specious at best. The French had never established a recognized title to the land east of the Mississippi. All the French could offer was their willingness to help the Americans realize their dubious claim.[8]

These discussions and disputes occurred during April 1803, which proved to be a month of rushed excitement for French and American diplomats alike. Livingston was overjoyed after all the delays

[6] Monroe to Madison, 17 September 1803, *Rives Collection*.
[7] Brown, ed., *The Autobiography of James Monroe*, 164.
[8] Dangerfield, *Chancellor Robert R. Livingston*, 364.

Illustrations (left to right): Francois Barbé-Marbois, from the collections of Louisiana State Museum; John Vanderlyn, *James Monroe* (1816), National Portrait Gallery, Smithsonian Institution; John Vanderlyn, *Robert R. Livingston* (1804), collection of the New York Historical Society. Color plates, page 172.

Illustrations: subsequent renderings of the final arrangements for the Louisiana Purchase. Left: Napoleon dictates plans for the Purchase to his ministers, Historic New Orleans Collection, accession no. 1974.25.10.64 Right: American and French diplomats sign the treaty, Historic New Orleans Collection, accession no. 1974.25.10.65. Color plates, page 173.

and frustrations he had encountered since arriving in France. On the other hand, these were difficult times for James Monroe. Convinced of Livingston's limitations and certain that his own participation was essential, Monroe was nonetheless forced to accept a secondary role. A back injury that incapacitated Monroe for several critical days in April contributed to his irritation. When Monroe finally felt strong enough to rejoin negotiations on April 1, he was compelled to invite Barbé-Marbois and Livingston to his apartment, where Monroe struggled to participate in negotiations while lying on a sofa.[9]

The negotiators finished their work on April 30. On May 2 they signed the official documents, their signatures backdated two days. In the treaty, France ceded all of its territory on the North American continent to the United States in exchange for $11.5 million and an American promise to annul $3.5 million in French debts to the United States. Nobody knew the exact boundaries of French Louisiana, but Livingston and Monroe were certain that they had doubled the size of the United States.

Throughout these weeks, Americans in the United States remained ignorant of events in Paris. Perhaps because they were busy, or perhaps because they wanted to wait until the negotiations were complete, neither Livingston nor Monroe informed Madison of the breakthrough with France. Madison had written to them several times since Monroe's departure in March. Unaware of the sudden change in Paris, Madison seemed increasingly out of step, still focusing on the acquisition of New Orleans and still suggesting tactics for working with an antagonistic French government.[10]

Livingston finally broke the silence on May 12, when he wrote a letter to Madison providing an overview of the sudden change in affairs.[11] The following day, Livingston and Monroe wrote a second letter informing Madison, the letter exclaiming that "we have the pleasure to transmit to you...a Treaty which we have concluded with the french Republic for the Purchase & Cession of Louisiana." They presented a united front as they explained why they had strayed so far

---

[9] Ammon, *James Monroe*, 212.
[10] Madison to Monroe, 1 May 1803, *PJM-SS4*, 562-3.
[11] Livingston to Madison, 12 May 1803, *PJM-SS4*, 590-2.

from their mandate. "An acquisition of so great an extent was, we well know, not contemplated by our appointment," they explained, "but we are persuaded that the Circumstances and Considerations which induced us to make it, will justify us, in the measure, to our Government and Country."[12] Monroe claimed that control of New Orleans would have been cheap at twice the price. Besides, the United States could always sell the rest of Louisiana in the future or trade it for the Floridas and other concessions from Spain.[13]

So certain were they that the Louisiana Purchase would be popular at home that Livingston and Monroe were almost immediately consumed by a nasty contest for recognition. "On my arrival I found the credit and character of our nation very low," Livingston wrote. Of the French, he recalled, "I answered them sincerely in such a manner as to satisfy them that I meant to have no intrigue with its enemies. I carefully avoided all connection with them and in consequence of this began to acquire a degree of favor."[14] In other words, the Louisiana Purchase was *Livingston's* doing. Monroe disagreed. "I sincerely wish my colleague [Livingston] to derive all the advantage and Credit which his exertion & intention entitle him to, but the transaction ought to rest on its own ground, as a memorable incident in our history." In other words, the Purchase was *Monroe's* doing.

Monroe left Paris in July 1803 to assume the post of minister to Great Britain. But his distance across the English Channel did little to quell his animosity toward Livingston. Nor was the conflict limited to the two diplomats. The dispute radiated outward, with friends taking intransigent sides on the matter. An infuriated Jefferson confided to Madison, "A more disgusting correspondence between men of sense...I have never read."[15]

Monroe and Livingston both considered themselves responsible for resolving the Mississippi Crisis. Of course, neither man was right. The Louisiana Purchase came about because Napoleon Bonaparte wanted to dispense with a colony, which, after his defeat on Saint-

---

[12] Monroe and Livingston to Madison, 13 May 1803, *PJM-SS4*, 601-6.
[13] Monroe to Madison, 14 May 1803, *PJM-PS4*, 610-5. See also Monroe to Jefferson, 18 May 1803, *Jefferson Papers*, Reel 45.
[14] Livingston to Madison, 12 May 1803, *PJM-SS4*, 591.
[15] Jefferson to Madison, 18 August 1804, *Jefferson Papers*, Reel 46. See also Ammon, *James Monroe*, 215-20; Dangerfield, *Chancellor Robert R. Livingston*, 376-7, 386-7.

Domingue, had lost its value. Whether Monroe and Livingston were aware of their secondary role in the sale of Louisiana is impossible to tell. They certainly never admitted as much. What remains clear is that both men considered the Purchase an unprecedented diplomatic success and neither would accept anything less than the lion's share of fame.

And what of the revolutionaries on Saint-Domingue? They abandoned their claims of loyalty to France, and in 1804 declared themselves citizens of Haiti, the second independent republic in the Americas. The United States government had no congratulations to offer, nor was the United States appreciative of the role the Haitians played in resolving the Mississippi Crisis. To the contrary, the Jefferson Administration refused to acknowledge Haiti, instead isolating the new independent republic both politically and diplomatically. Jefferson had two purposes in mind: to punish the slaves for overthrowing their masters and to prevent American slaves from aspiring to this example of freedom in the Caribbean. The Haitians struggled to create their own society despite the considerable pressure exerted by their massive neighbor on the American mainland.[16]

Whites fled Saint-Domingue, unwilling to live in a republic dominated by their former slaves or by the free people of color who had endured legal inequality to free whites. The white migration began in the 1790's, but surged in 1803. The largest number of refugees chose Cuba because it was nearby, but also because the island hosted a familiar plantation system. Others chose the United States, many of them entering through the port city of Charleston, South Carolina. Still more chose Louisiana. At the time, they believed they were moving to a French culture, which, under Spanish colonial rule, seemed immune from the revolutionary changes sweeping the French empire. Within months of their arrival, the refugees received news of the Louisiana Purchase and suddenly found themselves transformed from Spanish subjects to American citizens.

---

[16] Mathewson, "Jefferson and Haiti," 238-45; Onuf, "'To Declare Them a Free and Independent People,'" 37-8.

CHAPTER SIX

"You Were Justified by the Solid Reasons"

The Saint-Domingue refugees were not the only ones surprised by the Louisiana Purchase. So, too, were the Americans. The immediate reaction in the United States was one of relief. News reached Washington just as residents were preparing to celebrate the Fourth of July. On July 5, 1803, with Washington returning to business after celebrating the twenty-seventh anniversary of independence, Jefferson was at work in the President's House. Congress was out of session, and in such a new town, the departure of the Legislature made Washington seem deserted.

From his office in the President's House, Jefferson composed a letter to his son-in-law, Thomas Mann Randolph. Jefferson informed him that American negotiators had "signed a treaty with France, ceding to us the island of N. Orleans and all of Louisiana...This removes from us the greatest source of danger to our peace."[1] Just as the timing of the Louisiana Purchase can be misleading, so, too, can Jefferson's exuberant letter to Randolph. Jefferson was not pleased because the United States had acquired a vast new western frontier. He was pleased because negotiators had peacefully resolved the Mississippi Crisis in a way that secured American control over the Mississippi River.

For all Jefferson's pleasure at the resolution to the Mississippi Crisis, he immediately appreciated the ramifications of the Louisiana Purchase that France imposed on the United States. Rather than a small, strategic spit of land at the mouth of the Mississippi, his diplomats pledged the United States to buy millions of acres stretching from the Gulf of Mexico to Canada, from the Mississippi River to the

---

[1] Thomas Jefferson to Thomas Mann Randolph, 5 July 1803, *Jefferson Papers*, Reel 46.

Rocky Mountains. Such an acquisition may have satisfied Jefferson's most ambitious fantasies, but the president still focused on his earlier goals of securing American control over the Mouth of the Mississippi. The downside was that many American policymakers worried Louisiana would be impossible to govern and would be an easy target for European nations prepared to take control of the Mississippi by force.

These challenges do not mean that Jefferson and his advisors could find ways to accommodate the Louisiana Purchase. For example, no sooner did news of the Purchase reach the United States than Madison rushed a letter to Livingston and Monroe absolving them of any wrongdoing. "In concurring with the disposition of the French Government to treat for the whole of Louisiana, altho' the western part of it was not embraced by your powers, you were justified by the solid reasons which you give for it."[2] Still, it was a difficult fit. Jefferson and Madison worried about how to govern and defend what Monroe and Livingston had called "an acquisition of so great an extent."

Besides, like all sales, the Louisiana Purchase came with plenty of strings attached. The treaty guaranteed most favored trading status for French merchantmen entering New Orleans. It required the United States to extend full citizenship to all residents of Louisiana. It forced American officials to govern a territory about which they knew practically nothing. These provisions imposed unprecedented burdens on the nation's domestic, as well as foreign, policies.

Worse still was the news from Madrid. The Spanish were infuriated by the Purchase, particularly because the Treaty of San Ildefonso included a French pledge not to sell Louisiana to a third party. Spanish duplicity in breaking the Treaty of San Lorenzo now came back to haunt them as they faced similar betrayal at the hands of Napoleon. Unable to preserve their claim to Louisiana, the Spanish refused to surrender the Floridas.

Some of Jefferson's allies urged him to trade most of Louisiana

---

[2] Madison to Livingston and Monroe, 29 July 1803, *James Madison: Writings*, 671.

for the Floridas, and Jefferson gave serious consideration to that option. Reselling Louisiana was still on the table in 1807, when Congress appropriated $2 million for the administration to cultivate French assistance in acquiring the Floridas. Congress was intentionally vague on how the administration should use this money.[3] The Louisiana Purchase bound the United States to purchase *all* of Louisiana, which left the administration with little room to maneuver. Napoleon imposed this rule to guarantee that no other European power would control North America. Napoleon wanted to make certain that Louisiana would remain part of the United States.

In addition to ongoing international concerns, the Louisiana Purchase also posed serious questions within the United States. Was it constitutional to enlarge national boundaries? Critics charged that the administration had exceeded its constitutional prerogatives. Jefferson even drafted a series of constitutional amendments explicitly extending American sovereignty to include Louisiana. Madison was silent on the matter, which is striking. He had a central role in writing the Constitution but expressed no qualms about Louisiana. Jefferson and Madison eventually dismissed the constitutional objections, but they were forced to acknowledge that other thoughtful Americans had legitimate reasons to question the administration's actions. As Jefferson wrote to his friend and confidante, Kentucky Senator John Breckinridge, "This treaty must of course be laid before both Houses, because both have important functions to exercise respecting it."[4] This was a profound admission on the President's part. He recognized that the Louisiana Purchase was more than just a treaty with a foreign power. The treaty had reconstituted the United States.

In the fall of 1803, Jefferson and his cabinet members turned their attention to practical matters. First among these was the problem of cost. The federal treasury simply did not have $11.5 million, the amount the United States needed to pay France. Nor was there an American bank that could loan the government so much money.

Worse still, public funds seemed likely to decrease. In 1803 the

---

[3] Tucker and Hendrickson, *Empire of Liberty*, 148-54
[4] Jefferson to John Breckinridge, 12 August 1803, *Jefferson Papers*, Reel 46.

"YOU WERE JUSTIFIED BY THE SOLID REASONS"

federal government still raised most of its revenues from duties on foreign imports and from the sale of western lands. The possibility of renewed war in Europe threatened to reduce imports as European merchantmen fell victim to warships and privateers. Taxes were not a viable option to overcome the shortfall of government revenue. The Revolution had convinced many Americans that burdensome taxes constituted the first step on the road to tyranny. The federal government would also have to foot the bill for the government of Louisiana, a cost that would eventually exceeded the price tag for the Louisiana Purchase itself. While the government might eventually be able to sell the land it acquired from Louisiana through sale to land speculators or individual settlers, Jefferson needed to raise the $11.5 million immediately.[5]

Responsibility for financing the Louisiana Purchase fell on the narrow shoulders of Albert Gallatin, the secretary of the treasury. Gallatin ranked alongside Madison as one of the president's closest advisors, despite the fact that he was a newcomer to the United States and his adopted home was not even Virginia, where Jefferson found his most trusted associates. Born in Switzerland, speaking English with a thick French accent, Gallatin was nineteen years old when he immigrated to America in 1780. He settled in Pennsylvania, and by 1795 represented the state's western district in the House of Representatives. During the political turmoil of the 1790's, Gallatin quickly emerged as the chief economic thinker within Jefferson's coalition. In 1801, Jefferson asked him to take charge of the treasury, a position for which he was particularly well suited.

Through thirteen years at the Treasury Department, Gallatin struggled to convert the vague theories of Jeffersonian Republicanism into a viable economic policy. In 1803, that task meant raising a lot of money without upsetting the economy or imposing new taxes. The solution—first proposed by the French—proved as original as it was ingenious. Negotiators arranged financing through Hope & Company, a Dutch bank, and the British financial giant of the House of Baring.

---

[5] Bailyn, *The Ideological Origins of the American Revolution*, 209-11, 233-5.

The two banks would issue stock to the United States. The federal government in turn would deliver the stock to France once Louisiana was in American hands.

Gallatin met with Alexander Baring to complete the deal, creating a structure for issuing and eventually repaying the stock.[6] The European banking institutions had the financial resources, the international credit, and the experience that was lacking in the United States. The irony was that the United States was going in debt to a British institution at a time when Anglo-American relations were disintegrating, and France and Britain were preparing to go to war. This fact was not lost on some Americans, who criticized Jefferson for mortgaging the country to Great Britain in order to buy Louisiana from France.

Gallatin's primary objective as secretary of the treasury was to eliminate the federal debt. But, like Jefferson, he believed that debt retirement was not an end in itself. Debt retirement was only one of a number of ways to foster a free and prosperous republic. Access to credit, land, and trade were equally important. As a result, Gallatin was an avid supporter of the Louisiana Purchase. He believed the Purchase would promote harmony and progress throughout the West by securing the ability of American settlers to trade down the Mississippi River. Rejecting the Louisiana Purchase might have expedited the liquidation of American debt, but Gallatin and others concluded that benefit would come at the cost of tremendous threats to the nation's survival.[7]

What now seems like a simple stock transfer was in fact an elaborate process made all the more complicated by the delays of nineteenth-century transportation. Gallatin busied himself with the details. By August 1803, for example, he was writing to Philadelphia "in order to have the proper paper, copper-plate engravings, and other devices necessary to prevent counterfeits." To make the stock a viable offering, Gallatin decided that shares should be worth no more than a thousand dollars. He eventually opted for an issue of 11,250 shares,

---

[6] Walters, *Albert Gallatin*, 153-4.
[7] McCoy, *The Elusive Republic*, 180-1, 231; Sloan, *Principle and Interest*, 194-5, 204-5, 223-4.

"YOU WERE JUSTIFIED BY THE SOLID REASONS"

each of which required an individual signature and the subsequent paperwork of being "compared, checked, &c." Gallatin awaited the arrival of Alexander Baring before they completed the process, and then the United States would dispatch the shares to Livingston for final delivery to the French government. Gallatin warned Jefferson that all of these factors might yet delay the actual sale of Louisiana, assuring the president that "you may, however, rely on my exertions, and that every means which may accelerate the completion of the stock shall be adopted."[8]

Gallatin was under considerable pressure to get the finances in order. The Senate approved the Louisiana Purchase in October 1803, followed soon by an equally important vote by both Houses extending the reach of the federal government to include Louisiana.[9] Statements of outright criticism were few and far between. Whatever the shortcomings of the Louisiana Purchase, most Americans were overjoyed at the prospect of resolving the Mississippi Crisis in America's favor without resorting to war.[10] But public support focused on the Mississippi Crisis, repeating the sentiments that Jefferson expressed in his letter to Thomas Mann Randolph. "That the *United States* must possess the control of the navigation of the *Mississippi*, was stated as a settled and established point," wrote one pamphleteer, Samuel Brazer. "All parties agreed in the importance of the acquisition, and differed only in the means of securing it." That the United States had acquired additional land was also to be celebrated, but Brazer devoted most of his comments to exalting the administration for settling the Mississippi Crisis through peaceful means.[11] David Ramsay made the same point in a lecture he delivered in Charleston the following spring. "In other countries...seas have been crimsoned with human blood in the attack and defence of a few acres...but we have gained possession of this invaluable country, without imposition of any new taxes."[12]

As Gallatin completed the financing, Jefferson and Madison prepared the United States to take charge in Louisiana. The treaty

---

[8] Albert Gallatin to Jefferson, 31 August 1803, *Writings of Gallatin*, I: 146-7.
[9] *Statutes at Large*, II: 15.
[10] Deen, "Public Response to the Louisiana Purchase."
[11] Brazer, *Address in Commemoration of the Cession of Louisiana*, 7-8.
[12] Ramsay, *An Oration on the Cession of Louisiana to the United States*, 8.

mandated a complicated game of administrative musical chairs. French officials would eject the Spanish caretakers and resume direct administration. This would enable France to surrender Louisiana to the United States without Spanish interference.

Pierre Clément Laussat arrived in New Orleans to orchestrate the transfer. On November 30, 1803, Laussat restored French rule in Lower Louisiana for the briefest of times. On December 20, Laussat surrendered New Orleans to two American commissioners, William C.C. Claiborne and General James Wilkinson. It was during his trip from the Mississippi Territory to New Orleans in preparation for this event that Claiborne wrote his September 29 letter to Madison warning of the problems he expected to encounter. Despite these misgivings, Claiborne settled in to stay when Jefferson appointed him territorial governor the following spring. Three months after Claiborne and Wilkinson took charge in New Orleans, Captain Amos Stoddard met Carlos DeLassus in St. Louis. In a brief ceremony, the Spanish governor signed over control of Upper Louisiana and European colonial rule came to an end.[13]

By the end of 1803, the Louisiana Purchase seemed settled. Congress had approved the treaty. The United States was in charge of the new territory. The financing was at last in place. Many Americans believed their diplomatic problems in the Southwest were finally over. They could not have been more wrong.

---

[13] Claiborne to Jefferson, 20 December 1803, *Jefferson Papers*, 47; Claiborne to Madison, 20 December 1804, *Claiborne Letterbooks*, I: 306-7; James Wilkinson to Amos Stoddard, 23 January 1804, *Letters Received, Registered Series*, 2: W-204; Claiborne to Pierre Clement Laussat, 13 April 1804, in *Claiborne Letterbooks*, II.

"YOU WERE JUSTIFIED BY THE SOLID REASONS"

Chapter Seven
"The Character of the Country"

Americans soon realized it was not just the "Great Struggling Town" of New Orleans they had purchased. But the exact dimensions of what the United States had bought from France remained a mystery. Both the boundaries and the inhabitants of Louisiana would be the subject of unending dispute in the years that followed. Indeed, the Louisiana Purchase did not end in 1803 because so few people agreed on what Louisiana actually was.

Looking back almost two centuries later, it is easy to recognize that the Louisiana Purchase provided untold opportunities and resources for the United States. In 1803, however, the advantages of such an acquisition were far more difficult to see. Members of the Jefferson Administration expected unprecedented costs from governing Louisiana. They expected ongoing diplomatic disputes. The mysteries and uncertainties of the land itself only magnified these concerns. In the years after 1803, Americans struggled to establish a definition of Louisiana that fulfilled their own needs.

Nobody felt the pressure that came with the Purchase more profoundly than Jefferson and Madison. They worked hard to settle both the foreign and domestic residue of the Purchase and to determine exactly what people would mean when they spoke of "Louisiana." Jefferson's own scientific interest in North America was a low priority in 1803 for the President and his secretary of state. Both men were far more concerned with settling the boundaries of Louisiana against the claims of European powers. They also worried that the absence of information on who lived in Louisiana—whether European, African, or Native American—might preclude the United

States from creating a government for its vast new western frontier.

So the two men set out to create a map. Such a map would satisfy both foreign and domestic goals, for it would enable the United States to negotiate with confidence overseas while working with confidence at home on the difficult process of organizing the residents of Louisiana. Jefferson and Madison had no way of knowing they had started a task that would take over a decade to finish. That mapmaking process would prove integrally connected to a broader effort to define Louisiana and establish unchallenged American sovereignty.

Jefferson and Madison did not limit themselves to Louisiana's geographical boundaries. Federal policymakers believed that their ignorance of the North American West prevented them from creating an effective government beyond the Mississippi. As a result, they were eager to learn who lived in Louisiana, a necessary first step to determining how Louisiana would fit into an expanded United States. In the summer of 1803, Jefferson dispatched a series of queries to the few contacts he had in the Mississippi Valley. As much as any document, the queries showed how much Jefferson and Madison were concerned not only with the geographical boundaries of Louisiana, but also with its human contents. For example, question eight asked, "On what footing is the church and the clergy?" while question nine sought information "on the population of the Province distinguished between white and black, but excluding Indians."[1]

While they waited for a response, Jefferson and Madison explored the evidence already available to them. They ransacked their libraries and pestered friends for information on Louisiana. Voracious readers, Jefferson and Madison poured through the accounts of European explorers and scrutinized European land grants. They left no record indicating whether they pulled these books from the shelves of Monticello or Montpelier, Madison's Virginia plantation, or whether they found them in Washington. Jefferson and Madison used these books in the same way any modern researcher would. They hoped the

---

[1] Jefferson to Daniel Clark, 17 July 1803, *Jefferson Papers* Reel 46; Jefferson to William Dunbar, 17 July 1803, *Jefferson Papers* Reel 46.

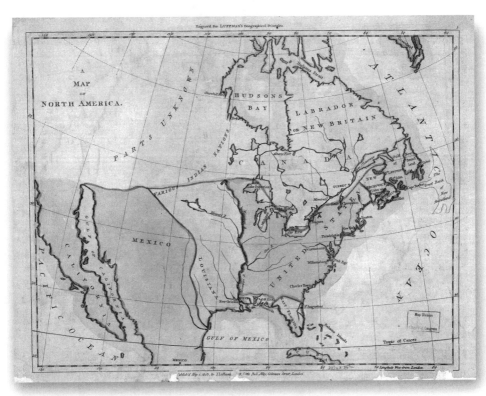

Illustrations: John Luffman, *A Map of North America*, (London: 1803), Geography and Map Division, courtesy of the Library of Congress. Color plate, page 174.

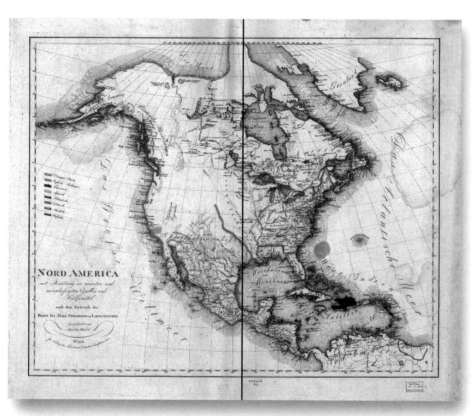

Joseph Marx Liechtenstern, *Nord America mit Benützung der neuesten and zuverlaessigsten Quellen und Hülfsmittel,* (1804). John Luffman's 1803 map used vague geographic references to indicate the boundaries of the United States, Louisiana, and Mexico. Liechtenstern's map provided a more detailed description of landscape, but with only a single line to indicate the western boundary of Louisiana and no northern terminus. Geography and Map Division, Library of Congress. Color plate, page 175.

"THE CHARACTER OF THE COUNTRY"

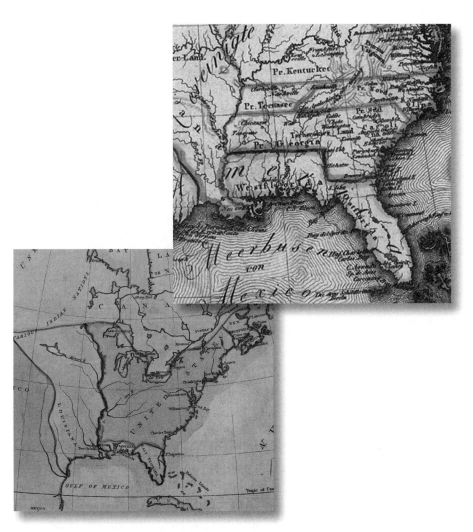

A closeup of the two maps reveals not only the absence of geographic information, but also the range of boundaries that people associated with Louisiana. The two maps propose substantially different western boundaries, as well different conceptions of West Florida. Both maps designed the Floridas as political entities distinct from Louisiana.

history of Louisiana would provide the answers they wanted to difficult boundary questions.[2]

In the end, Jefferson and Madison produced three remarkable documents: "An inquiry concerning the northern Boundary of Canada and Louisiana," "An examination into the boundaries of Louisiana," and "Chronological series of facts relative to Louisiana." In the first two documents, they attempted to determine the geographical limits of Louisiana. No detail was too small. Jefferson and Madison included minor rivers, streams, and valleys. The Chronology, written in Jefferson's hand, was even more extraordinary. Citing author, chapter, and page, Jefferson recorded the sources of his understanding of Louisiana. This sort of rigorous citation was extremely rare for published histories in the early nineteenth century, let alone internal memoranda. Jefferson discussed the colonial regimes and the migration patterns that implanted a population of white settlers and black slaves, thoroughly researching and documenting the history of Louisiana.[3]

The first trickle of information in response to their questions raised additional questions. Jefferson had asked how many people lived in Louisiana. Nobody knew. Many of the respondents simply copied the information from the 1785 Spanish census, which reported close to 42,000 people in Upper and Lower Louisiana: 20,000 whites, 1,700 free people of color, 12,920 slaves, and close to 7,000 Indians. But several of these people questioned their own sources. Alternative estimates put the population of Louisiana anywhere from 40,000 to 100,000. Even statistics for New Orleans proved elusive. The official count was 8,056, but Daniel Clark, the American consul in the port city, claimed it was significantly higher.[4] Establishing a figure for the total Indian population proved even more difficult. Jefferson's correspondents offered wildly varying figures, all presented with the caveat that no source provided truly reliable estimates.[5]

Jefferson submitted this information to Congress, which soon released it to the public. In late 1803 various publishers began to print

---

[2] le Page du Pratz, *Histoire de la Louisiane;* Hennepin, *Description de la Louisiane;* Stiles, ed., *Joutel's Journal of La Salle's Last Voyage;* Hutchins, *An Historical Narrative and Topographical Description;* Tonti, et. al, *On the Discovery of the Mississippi* Du Pratz's history appeared in various editions. Although Jefferson and Madison were likely to have read the original French versions, English translations had been published as early as the 1770s. Hutchins' published his narrative in 1784. Jefferson referred to Tonti's chronicle, although the earliest publication date is absent from the 1844 edition.

"THE CHARACTER OF THE COUNTRY"

an informational booklet called *An Account of Louisiana*. This document recapitulated many of the points that newspapers had already pointed out. Most importantly, however, it acknowledged that "the precise boundaries of Louisiana...though very extensive, are at present involved in some obscurity."[6]

When it did not know specific facts, *An Account of Louisiana* exaggerated, telling of land so fertile that crops practically raised themselves. Even the *National Intelligencer,* a Washington newspaper that served as the voice of the Jeffersonian Republicans, contributed to the hoopla, running advertisements for a book that would establish "the character of the country" in Louisiana and describe the great wonders of the West. All these reports failed to bring policymakers any closer to a clear understanding of their new acquisition, and, to the administration it was becoming obvious they would have to learn more about Louisiana before they could govern it.[7]

What information they did have offered little consolation to American policymakers. For their research in 1803, Jefferson and Madison always returned to square one: did the numerous European land transfers mean that Louisiana included the Floridas? By the summer of 1803, even Jefferson and Madison had to admit that it probably did not. They had no doubt that Louisiana extended to the Rockies. Taken together, these facts created concern. The *absence* of a clear claim to West Florida left the United States vulnerable. Meanwhile, the *presence* of a vastly expanded union would force the administration to govern an area that might exceed the capacities of the federal government.

---

[3] "An inquiry concerning the Northern Boundary of Canada and Louisiana," Undated 1803 original from Madison to James Monroe, *Madison Papers*, Reel 8; The exact date and provenance of these documents remains uncertain. They no doubt emerged in response to the Treaty of Cession's vagueness on the issue of boundaries. The treaty simply transferred territorial authority from France to the United States, without delineating the precise limits of French territory. The only indication of the date is on Monroe's copy of the "inquiry," which is docketed with a receipt date of 13 February 1804. Monroe, the minister plenipotentiary, shifted his attention from Louisiana to the rising Anglo-American discord over neutral rights. Allowing for a one-month Transatlantic passage, it is unlikely that Madison dispatched the "inquiry" after the new year. Livingston received a letterpress copy of the "inquiry," which indicates that it was produced and mailed at the same time as Monroe's copy. The "Chronological series of facts" appears to be in Jefferson's handwriting. Another undated copy of the chronology appears in the *Jefferson Papers* Reel 47, in a collection of undated documents that the Library of Congress has attributed to 1803.

[4] Clark to Madison, 17 August 1803, *Consular Dispatches,* New Orleans, 1. Additional information arrived in Clark to Madison, 20 August 1803, *Consular Dispatches,* New Orleans, 1; Amos Stoddard to Jefferson, 3 June 1803, *Jefferson Papers* Reel 47. See also undated documents from 1803 in *Jefferson Papers* Reel 47.

[5] In addition to Clark's correspondence and the undated information in *Jefferson Papers* see "Extracts from the journal of Jean Baptiste Trudeau," *Jefferson Papers* Reel 47, in the section of undated documents. Trudeau worked for the Upper Missouri Company, and recorded this information in 1795-6. Jefferson enclosed the material in a 16 November 1803 letter to Meriwether Lewis, but did not indicate when he received the information.

[6] *An Account of Louisiana*

[7] *National Intelligencer* [Washington, DC], 18 January 1804.

Illustration: Jefferson's queries, *Thomas Jefferson Papers*, Library of Congress. Top: the full list of queries. Bottom: closeup of first four questions.

"THE CHARACTER OF THE COUNTRY"

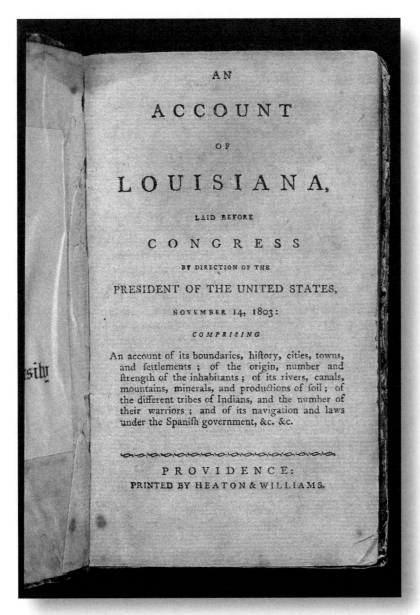

Illustration: From An Account of Louisiana (Providence: Heaton & Williams, 1803), courtesy of Special Collections, Washington University in St. Louis. Color plate, page 176.

In the years after 1803, Jefferson and Madison launched a campaign to resolve the problems posed by the Louisiana Purchase. They used their diplomatic and military resources to imagine boundaries for Louisiana that satisfied them. They dispatched a series of expeditions to traverse the continental interior to find out more about the people and land itself within Louisiana. And when it came to governing Louisiana, they drew on their experiences since Independence to build a federal apparatus of unprecedented size and power.

Diplomacy, exploration, and government dominated the agenda of the Jefferson Administration after 1803. To Jefferson and Madison, Congressional approval for the Louisiana Purchase was the beginning of a lengthy process to incorporate the new territory. That process would outlast Jefferson's own term in office.

CHAPTER EIGHT

"SPANISH CHAOS, FRENCH ACQUISITIVENESS, AND BRITISH AVARICE"

The Louisiana Purchase sent American diplomats scrambling. The diplomatic outreach occurred on four separate fronts as the United States reoriented its relationships with France, Spain, Great Britain, and the numerous Indians of the North American interior. Jefferson, Madison, and Monroe attempted to create the circumstances that would enable them to realize their diplomatic goals, and, once again, developments in Europe overshadowed their efforts. Try as they might to initiate favorable circumstances, over and over American leaders ended up responding to events. In the end, it was revolution and warfare in Europe—and in the Americas—that enabled Jefferson, Madison, and Monroe to uncover opportunities and realize their goals on the new western frontier.

With three of those partners—Spain, Britain, and the Indians—the Louisiana Purchase stimulated new tensions. In only one circumstance did it create immediate amity. The Louisiana Purchase settled affairs with France. Only two years after Jefferson had predicted war with France over New Orleans, the French imperial threat diminished. Napoleon remained a force in Europe, but the alarming language that Jefferson employed in 1802 and 1803 disappeared from the American diplomatic lexicon. The Louisiana Purchase and Haitian independence had stripped France of its power in the Americas.

Napoleon's aspirations in Europe were another story, and the Americans remained wary of France. The predictions of a renewed European war proved accurate. American policymakers immediately worried that the conflict might consume the United States. Even if it did not, it promised to create new restrictions on American trade in Europe. Nonetheless, the war helped to further remove France as a source of American diplomatic concern. Once France and Britain returned to arms only weeks after French and American diplomats signed the Louisiana Purchase, Napoleon was far too busy preserving alliances and confronting his enemies to worry about developments on the American side of the Atlantic.

The Indians of the continental interior filled the diplomatic vacuum left by France. During the 1780's and 1790's, the United States Army had already established control over the modern Midwest and portions of the Deep South. Tension and warfare continued on the American frontier within its pre-Louisiana Purchase borders, but the government in Washington had consolidated its power. With the Louisiana Purchase, the United States suddenly had to negotiate with dozens of new, unfamiliar tribes.[1]

Indians, in turn, found their own diplomatic world turned on its head by the Louisiana Purchase, and their reactions varied. After generations of experience with the French and Spanish, Indians of the North American interior suddenly found themselves confronted with the United States. The Indians of the Mississippi Valley adjusted their own foreign policies as contact with Americans increased. Some tribes found that the Purchase placed them at a distinct advantage. Located between two antagonistic nations—the United States and Spain—they soon recognized they could play both sides against one another to exploit conditions to preserve their own autonomy.

Nobody appreciated this situation better than Dehahuit, the Caddo chief (or Caddi) who wielded influence on the Texas-Louisiana border. Although there is no surviving record to document his birth, Dehahuit was born around 1760, two years after James Monroe. Like Monroe, Dehahuit struggled to advance his diplomatic agenda in a world of international tension. As he explained in an 1806 speech to William C.C. Claiborne, "If your nation has purchased what the French formerly possessed, you have purchased the country that we

---

[1] Dowd, *A Spirited Resistance*, 111-22; White, *The Middle Ground*, 382, 413-20.

occupy, and we regard you in the same light as we did them." This was a statement of peace. But it was also an assertion of sovereignty. Like other Indians of Louisiana, Dehahuit acknowledged the American claim to Louisiana, even allowing an American flag to fly in a Caddo village. But Dehahuit denied white claims that came at the cost of Indian autonomy.

Dehahuit succeeded, at least for a while. In the years following the Purchase, the Caddo used Spanish-American tensions to carve out a piece of territory called the "Neutral Ground." This narrow strip of land along the Texas-Louisiana border remained off limits to all whites except for a few designated Indian agents. Spanish, American, and Indian leaders went to great lengths to sustain the Neutral Ground because they saw distinct advantages to the agreement. The Neutral Ground was a buffer zone that would prevent violent encounters while negotiators struggled to resolve the boundaries of Louisiana.[2]

The Neutral Ground preserved Caddo autonomy even as the number of white settlers in the area continued to grow. American and Spanish military officials sent joint expeditions to remove white squatters, less from any altruistic concern for the Caddo than from the fear of an Indian war. As Colonel Thomas Cushing informed Secretary of War William Eustis in 1810, "Should you approve of the plan, and authorize a Co-operation on our part, an early check may be put to an evil which, if permitted to progress, may produce very injurious Consequences at a future day."[3] These officers had no love for the Caddo, but they feared an Indian war would drag the entire region into chaos. Indians accepted these brief incursions by white military forces as a small price to pay for removing the intruders. Any attempt by the Caddo to oust the whites might have led to white military reprisals. So why not let the white nations absorb the cost and the dangers? After all, it was their citizens who were causing the trouble.

The experience of the Caddo showed that Indians could benefit from the Louisiana Purchase if they knew how to negotiate with white officials. By contrast, the Indians of the Great Plains and the Rockies

---

[2] Smith, The Caddo Indians, 96-7; Weber, The Spanish Frontier in North America, 294-6; Nasatir, Borderland in Retreat, 3, 87-8, 115, 128-32.
[3] Thomas to William Eustis, 1 April 1810, Letters Received, Registered Series, 35: C-126.

had only limited contact with representatives of white nations and vice versa.[4] In an environment of uncertainty and distrust, the Indians of the Northern Plains hoped to establish the diplomatic flexibility they needed to respond to the dramatic changes occurring throughout North America. As Mandan chiefs told Jefferson and Secretary of War Henry Dearborn, "We feel entirely our happiness at this Day, since you tell us that we are welcome in the Grand lodge of prosperity. We perceive that we are numbered among your Most Cherished Children." Like Dehahuit, the Mandan chiefs were not surrendering to American sovereignty. While their status as "children" seemed to acknowledge a subordinate status, it also placed responsibilities on their "father," Thomas Jefferson.[5]

Jefferson and Madison knew that a stable diplomatic relationship with the Indians of Louisiana would convince competitors like Spain and Britain that the United States was actually governing Louisiana. Jefferson and Madison's attitudes toward Indians had hardened by 1803. Long before the Louisiana Purchase, they had come to believe Indians should accommodate themselves to the authority of the federal government. The United States would negotiate with Indians, but most American officials resented the autonomy of the Louisiana Indians. It was left to the Indians of the continental interior to look out for their own interests, and they did so by exploiting the tension among white nations. In the process, they were able to stave off American attempts to undermine their independence.[6]

In the complex statecraft of North America, diplomatic initiatives overlapped in numerous, confusing, and occasionally conflicting ways. Nowhere was this more true than in regard to Spain. For Indians, the boundary dispute between the United States and Spain often created ideal circumstances for Indians to build their diplomatic muscle and to preserve their independence. From the American perspective, relations with Spain posed one of the greatest threats to independence. The greatest problem for American policymakers was

---

[4] Jackson, *Thomas Jefferson & the Stony Mountains*, 170-3.
[5] Indian speech to Jefferson and Henry Dearborn, 4 January 1806, in Jackson, ed., *Letters of the Lewis and Clark Expedition*, I: 18.
[6] Sheehan, *Seeds of Extinction*, 159-63.

not the distant western boundary of Louisiana. Instead, Americans worried to no end after the Spanish made clear that *their* definition of Louisiana did not include the Floridas. Madison eventually decided that Spain's "obstinate and unfriendly" behavior toward the United States over Florida proved that it was a "violent and predatory" nation.[7]

In 1804 Jefferson and Madison dispatched Monroe to Spain, hopeful that their trusted negotiator would resolve the dispute. Monroe was in London at the time, having left Paris soon after the Louisiana Purchase to assume the post of U.S. Minister to Great Britain. He reached Madrid on New Year's Day, 1805, and informed the Spanish that, in exchange for a Spanish pledge to surrender West Florida, the United States would offer money or concessions on the western border of Louisiana. The Spanish would not budge. The Floridas were no less important to Spain than they were to the United States. Both countries saw the Floridas as a critical strategic outpost. Spanish policymakers believed that this small piece of land gave them control of the Gulf of Mexico, which, in turn, would protect their vital possessions in Central and South America.

When his mission to Spain failed to extend American sovereignty to the Floridas, Monroe shifted his diplomacy to England. He returned to London, but he was no more successful than he had been in Madrid. In 1807 Monroe abandoned his overseas work and returned to the United States. Writing to Virginia Senator William Branch Giles, Monroe confided, "it is painful to touch on" his experiences in Europe, adding, "I shod. Feel myself deficient in candour if I did not observe that at no period of my life was I subjected to more inquietude."[8]

Monroe's experience served as a reminder that Napoleon Bonaparte, and not Thomas Jefferson, had determined the Louisiana Purchase. Unlike the French, the Spanish had no compelling reason to abandon the Gulf Coast in 1805. Monroe had nothing to offer, nor did he have any leverage to exploit.[9] Jefferson never found a way to settle

---

[7] Madison to William C.C. Claiborne, 18 November 1805, Carter, IX: 533; Tucker and Hendrickson, *Empire of Liberty*, 148-54.
[8] Monroe to William Branch Giles, 30 April 1807, *Monroe Writings*, V: 5.
[9] Ammon, *James Monroe*, 15-47; Tucker and Hendrickson, *Empire of Liberty*, 150-4.

the border dispute to America's satisfaction. As Jefferson's second term came to an end, Spain still controlled the Floridas just east of New Orleans and the western boundary of Louisiana remained a subject of dispute.

Thomas Jefferson left Washington in 1809, exhausted by a lifetime in public office and eight difficult years as president. He was particularly dejected because Monroe had failed to reach an accord with Spain over the Floridas and, worse still, because Anglo-American tensions hit the boiling point. Jefferson imposed an embargo on all American trade in an attempt to force Britain to abandon its discriminatory trade practices. The results were disastrous. Far from hurting the British, the embargo only succeeded in devastating the American economy. More dispiriting to Jefferson was the fact that many Americans ignored the embargo, participating in a growing black market across the Atlantic and in Canada.

Although this experience left him deeply embittered, Jefferson took pleasure in his domestic victories. The Republicans commanded a growing majority over their Federalist opponents in both houses of Congress as well as in state legislatures, and Jefferson's handpicked successor, James Madison, won the 1808 presidential election. As far as Jefferson was concerned, Madison was the perfect choice, a president with expertise in both the executive and legislative branches of the federal government. As a young man, Madison helped shape the Constitution. Throughout much of the 1790's, he was a leading member of Congress and had organized the Jeffersonian opposition to the Federalists. When Jefferson came to power, he had orchestrated American foreign policy. "I salute you," Jefferson wrote to Madison soon after his friend moved into the President's House. The postmark on the letter was telling. Jefferson had retired yet again to Monticello, this time for good.[10]

As Madison assumed the presidency, he felt even more limited in his diplomatic options than he had as secretary of state. Where Madison himself had been an effective subordinate to Thomas

---

[10] Jefferson to Madison, 17 March 1809, *PJM-PS1*, 60.

Jefferson, Madison considered his own secretary of state, Robert Smith, both incompetent and disloyal. He had only offered Smith the post in order to satisfy influential Republicans. It seemed an effective political move, but it created considerable tension within the administration. Worse still were developments overseas that further prevented Madison from reaching a breakthrough with Spain. In 1808, Napoleon abandoned a decade and a half of treaties and agreements with Spain, invaded the Iberian Peninsula, and placed his own brother, Joseph Bonaparte, on the Spanish throne. The deposed monarch, Charles IV, abandoned Madrid and together with his advisors created a government-in-exile at Cadiz, a port city on the southwestern corner of Spain. The Cadiz government quickly signed an alliance with Great Britain. In a matter of weeks the entire tenor of the war in Europe changed, with profound ramifications for the Americas.

Relations between the United States and Spain, already strained, collapsed entirely as Madison concluded that the United States could not recognize either the Napoleon regime in Madrid or the monarchist government in Cadiz. Madison worried that neither government could claim legitimate rule and the tumult in Spain would spread to the Americas. Residents of Spanish America soon proclaimed their loyalty to Charles IV and began to negotiate separate treaties with their new ally, Great Britain.[10]

Madison could only conclude that the crisis revealed "Spanish chaos, French acquisitiveness, and British avarice."[11] As had been the case for years, his attention focused on West Florida, fearful that the collapse of the Spanish empire might now provide France and Britain with the pretext to establish a foothold on the Mississippi. This was exactly the situation Americans had feared during the Mississippi Crisis of 1802 and 1803, and the situation in 1809 served as a reminder that the Louisiana Purchase had failed to meet American needs.[12]

The trigger for change in the Gulf Coast eventually came not from Washington, Paris, or Madrid, but from the Gulf Coast itself. As

---

[10] *PJM-PS2*, 305-20; Weber, *The Spanish Frontier in North America*, 294-301.
[11] Madison to Jefferson, 19 October 1810, *PJM-PS2*, 585-6. He duplicated this phrase in Madison to John Armstrong, 19 October 1810, *PJM-PS2*, 597-9.
[12] "James Madison and the Collapse of the Spanish Empire," *PJM-PS2*, 305-20.

had been the case in Louisiana, the Spanish were content to let others settle West Florida so long as they accepted Spanish sovereignty. By 1810 the majority of West Florida's white residents were Anglo-Americans. With the collapse of the Spanish monarchy, a number of these residents near Baton Rouge formed a convention to secure greater control over local affairs. The West Florida Convention was an odd collection of wealthy planters and violent frontiersmen, some of whom were wanted in the United States *and* Spanish America for a variety of crimes.[13] In September 1810 the conventioneers declared themselves the government of an independent republic and immediately stormed the Spanish fort at Baton Rouge. Madison responded on October 27, 1810, by ordering the annexation of West Florida. He reasserted the American claim to West Florida under the Louisiana Purchase, saying, "a crisis has at length arrived subversive of the order of things under the Spanish authorities, whereby a failure of the United States to take...[West Florida] into its possession may lead to events ultimately contravening the views of both parties."[14]

American troops descended on the Gulf Coast in December 1810, and, by the start of the new year, the United States had subdued the convention and expelled the Spanish from Baton Rouge. The dream of so many Americans since Independence—control of the mouth of the Mississippi—had come true. Jefferson and Madison's vision of a peaceful negotiation gave way to military power. Spanish forces retreated to Mobile while representatives from the monarchist government in Cadiz launched half-hearted attempts to restore their sovereignty. There was little they could do given their circumstances.[15]

Madison now focused his attention on the rest of West Florida, running from Mobile to Pensacola. His ally in that effort was none other than James Monroe, who joined the cabinet in 1811 as secretary of state when Madison ejected Robert Smith. There was no pretext like the West Florida Convention to validate further American annexation. But just as a French war against Spain enabled Madison to seize the area around Baton Rouge in 1810, a British war with the

---

[13] Cox, *The West Florida Controversy*, 312-436.
[14] Madison, Presidential Proclamation, 27 October 1810, *PJM-PS2*, 595.
[15] Louis de Onìs to Alexander Dallas, 4 December 1810, *Miscellaneous Letters*, XXIII; Dallas to Smith, *Miscellaneous Letters*, XXIII; Cox, *the West Florida Controversy*, 608-34.

"SPANISH CHAOS, FRENCH ACQUISITIVENESS, AND BRITISH AVARICE"

United States would provide the circumstances in which he could move on the rest of West Florida.

Of course, securing the Floridas was not the reason why James Madison asked Congress to declare war against Great Britain in 1812. The War of 1812 was instead the product of long-simmering disputes between the United States and Great Britain. And yet the War of 1812 deserves some explaining not only because it would eventually have a profound effect on the struggle to define Louisiana, but also because the roots of that war serve as a reminder of the reasons why the administration sought the Louisiana Purchase and why Americans continued to worry about Louisiana after 1803. The impressment of American seamen into the Royal Navy—the most famous source of Anglo-American discord—was in fact less important to most Americans than a British policy which seemed to stifle American trade.

Anglo-American commercial disputes dating back to the 1780s were the primary cause of the War of 1812. No sooner did Britain acknowledge American independence than the British government excluded American merchants from some of the most lucrative trading routes in the Atlantic. This began as a form of commercial competition flavored with a healthy dose of British venom for the former colonies. The policy became part of British strategic planning in the 1790's. As the war with France dragged on, the British imposed a blockade on continental Europe that eventually excluded all vessels, including Americans. British efforts to exclude American trade from the Caribbean and from Europe constituted a threat much like foreign control over the Mississippi.[16]

Madison hoped a quick war would resolve the situation. The United States would seize the Canadian maritime provinces and hold them hostage in exchange for a new British policy free of the old restrictions. Madison believed Britain was so utterly dependent on Canada for vital resources that officials in London would surrender. Like the Louisiana Purchase, this was not a campaign of territorial

---

[16] Perkins, *Prologue to War*; Spivak, *Jefferson's English Crisis*; Stagg, "James Madison and the Coercion of Great Britain."

acquisition. Instead, as in 1803, Americans sought limited territorial goals in order to achieve broader diplomatic goals.[17]

In 1812, the president's allies considered his plan optimistic. It would be more accurate to call it unrealistic. The war quickly spiraled out of control, dragged on for two-and-a-half years, and spread across the American coastline and the U.S.-Canadian border.[18] While Madison lamented this state of affairs, he also realized these circumstances might settle affairs in West Florida. Back in 1810 Madison had decided against moving beyond Baton Rouge because he worried the British would come to Spain's aid. Now he had no such qualms and, in 1813, American troops seized Mobile.[19]

The following year, Andrew Jackson launched an undeclared war against the Creek Indians of the Gulf Coast. Creek warriors often sought refuge on Spanish soil. Jackson accused the Spanish governor of Pensacola, Gonzales Marinque, of interfering in American affairs. When Marinque fired off a terse reply, Jackson claimed to have "insult, upon insult to my government, and the greatest disrespect for myself...You have thrown the gauntlet, and I take it up." The irascible Tennessean punished Spain by seizing its outpost. Jackson left behind a shattered Pensacola fortress the Spanish had neither the manpower nor the finances to rebuild.[20]

By the end of 1814, the United States controlled the Gulf Coast from Baton Rouge to Pensacola. War with Britain and Jackson's moment of pique had created conditions that enabled the United States to accomplish Monroe and Livingston's unfinished business. These victories took advantage of the last stages of the French occupation of Spain. In 1814 British troops and Spanish guerillas drove Napoleon from the Iberian Peninsula and restored the monarchy. But the Spanish government was far too busy re-establishing its authority in its Central and South American colonies to worry about the Floridas. The beleaguered Spanish lacked the resources to launch a counterattack on the Gulf Coast.

---

[17] Stagg, *Mr. Madison's War*, 16-47.
[18] Stagg, *Mr. Madison's War*, 130-76.
[19] Monroe to Albert Gallatin, 5 May 1813, *Monroe Writings*, V: 252-4; Monroe to Gallatin, 6 May 1813, *Monroe Writings*, V: 259; Monroe to John Quincy Adams, 10 December 1815, *Monroe Writings*, V: 380-2. The importance that Monroe (and Madison for matter) attached to Spanish "connivance" in the British war effort appears in Monroe to Jackson, 27 September 1814, *Monroe Writings*, V: 296-7.

The Southern frontier was the site of the last major battle of the War of 1812, an ironic twist to a war Madison had planned to fight in the North. On January 8, 1815, a combination of American regulars, Louisiana militiamen, Kentucky and Tennessee volunteers, Indians, and free men of color handed the British a crushing defeat on the marshy fields outside New Orleans. The Battle of New Orleans actually occurred two weeks *after* American and British negotiators had signed a peace treaty at the French town of Ghent.

The Treaty of Ghent ended the war, provided some satisfaction for American commercial interests, but still did not guarantee a permanent resolution to the American fear that European powers could restrict American trade. It would require changes in Europe, and those changes coincided with peace with North America. In 1814 Napoleon was defeated and banished to the Mediterranean island of Elba. He made a brief attempt to reclaim power in 1815 and went into final exile at St. Helena, an island in the middle of the Atlantic. Two decades of European war had finally come to an end.

It is impossible to overestimate the significance of this change in Europe. With Napoleon deposed, the British relaxed their limitations on American trade and eliminated the impressment of American sailors.[21] With the Spanish crown restored, the United States had a viable negotiating partner in Madrid.

Better still, the Spanish seemed eager to reach a settlement. Residents of Spanish America had remained loyal to the crown during the Napoleonic War, but now they demanded reform. The Spanish worried that the United States might aid the renegades unless the two nations could establish friendly relations.[22] In 1815 Monroe informed the Senate Military Committee that, "With Spain our affairs are yet unsettled." Nonetheless, he believed, "The period is perhaps arrived when it may be practicable to settle on just and honorable conditions."[23] In 1816 Madison informed Secretary of War William Crawford, "an invasion by a Spanish force at the present period might be pronounced a mere chimoera."[24] By the time Madison retired in

<hr/>

[20] Jackson to Gonzales Manrique, 9 September 1814, *Papers of Andrew Jackson,* III: 130; Stagg, *Mr. Madison's War,* 490.
[21] Perkins, *Castlereagh and Adams;* Stagg, *Mr. Madison's War,* 501-17.
[22] Lewis, *The American Union and the Problem of Neighborhood,* 116-25; Weeks, *John Quincy Adams and American Global Empire.*
[23] Monroe to Military Committee of the Senate, 22 February 1815, *Monroe Writings,* V: 323-4.

1817, he was confident the United States and Spain were finally approaching a resolution to the disputes left by the Louisiana Purchase. Like Jefferson, Madison found two terms an exhausting experience. Also like Jefferson, he returned to his Virginia plantation after surrendering the presidency to his secretary of state, James Monroe.[25]

Monroe was optimistic as he assumed office. The American economy flourished with the peace in Europe. The Federalists were no longer dangerous opponents and had lost most of their constituency by 1817. Monroe and his fellow Jeffersonian Republicans were free to determine their own policies. Monroe soon proclaimed an Era of Good Feelings, in which Americans enjoyed economic prosperity and political tranquility.

Settling the boundaries of Louisiana was at the top of Monroe's diplomatic agenda. He now turned to Secretary of State John Quincy Adams, one of the most experienced diplomats in the country. Adams was nine years old when he first accompanied his father, John Adams, to Europe. At age fourteen in 1781, Adams became the private secretary and interpreter for the American envoy to Russia. He served as a diplomat in the Netherlands and Prussia before returning to Russia as the American envoy. Later, as American minister to Great Britain, Adams had helped negotiate the end of the War of 1812. Now he was ready to serve as Monroe's secretary of state.

In 1803, when Monroe signed the Louisiana Purchase, Adams was a Senator from Massachusetts who expressed reservations about the treaty. In 1819, however, Adams succeeded where Jefferson, Madison, and Monroe had failed, negotiating a treaty with Spain to establish the western boundary of Louisiana and grant the United States authority over the Floridas. Called the Transcontinental Treaty, the Senate approved the agreement two years later.

The Transcontinental Treaty came in the midst of broader changes that ended the diplomatic world that shaped the attitudes of

---

[24] Madison to William Crawford, 23 September 1816, *Madison Writings*, 22-3.
[25] Drew R. McCoy, *The Last of the Fathers*; Ketcham, *James Madison*, 613-6.

Jefferson, Madison, and Monroe. The same year negotiators completed the Transcontinental Treaty, the American economy suffered a devastating collapse. The Panic of 1819 left thousands of Americans destitute and disrupted the economy for years. Equally important, it led many Americans to demand that the federal government focus on domestic problems rather than foreign affairs.

Overseas, the person who had dictated the terms of the Louisiana Purchase, Napoleon Bonaparte, died in 1821. Anglo-American tension, a constant in American foreign policy since 1776, was giving way to a new relationship which, if not friendly, was at least amicable. Spain was disappearing from the diplomatic landscape. Even as Spain settled affairs with the United States, it was rapidly losing control over its American colonies. Spanish diplomats finalized the Transcontinental Treaty at the same time other Spanish leaders were forced to acknowledge the independence of Mexico.

When Monroe took up the question of Mexican independence, the old order in the Americas was gone for good. The Transcontinental Treaty was already in place. Indeed, Monroe postponed considering Mexican independence until he had a treaty that stated once and for all what the United States had bought from France in 1803. Whatever came of American relations with Mexico, Monroe would not consider relinquishing any of the territory it had taken so long to acquire. Eighteen years after accepting the assignment to Paris, Monroe could also take confidence in the fact that the Louisiana Purchase was finally settled.[26]

---

[26] Lewis, *The American Union and the Problem of Neighborhood*, 152-4.

CHAPTER NINE

"THE GRAND EXCURSION"

The Transcontinental Treaty was more than a document. It was a map. The treaty specified the boundaries of Louisiana, using natural landmarks (mostly rivers) as well as longitude and latitude. But establishing those points of reference rested on an accurate survey of the North American interior. It was not that the Spanish or the Americans had refused to provide that survey to the other party before 1819. Such a survey simply did not exist. As a result, in 1803 the simple act of envisioning Louisiana was no simple task.

Although cartographers had attempted to create maps of western North America, their maps all had their limitations and, worse still, often conflicted with one another.[1] Within a decade, however, men and women throughout the United States believed they knew what they had purchased from France. There was more at stake than the diplomatic settlement of Louisiana's borders. Americans could not believe that Louisiana was truly theirs until they knew the dimensions and the character of the new land they had acquired.

Bringing Louisiana into focus was a coordinated effort that involved people throughout the country. Exploring Louisiana is a tale of high adventure, but it also provides lessons in the workings of the federal government, insights into science in the Age of the Enlightenment, and the means to understand a world beset by international tensions. While American explorers struggled to gather information on the West, government officials from the East provided funding, resources, and training. Meanwhile, Indians initiated their own exploration. Various Indian tribes encountered American expedition after American expedition, and they sought to understand

---

[1] Allen, "Geographical Knowledge & American Images of the Louisiana Territory."

Americans just as Americans struggled to understand them.

Jefferson and Madison sought a map of Louisiana that would settle once and for all the boundaries of Louisiana. This was a simple diplomatic concern. Maps determined ownership, whether for neighbors, states, or nations. Beyond this immediate concern, however, Jefferson and Madison knew that if Americans ever settled in Louisiana, they would need accurate surveys to prevent the sort of nasty and occasionally violent disputes that were all too common on American frontiers.[2]

But Jefferson and Madison also had less pragmatic reasons for studying geography. They wanted to know where they stood, both literally and figuratively. Americans found that maps and travel accounts enabled them to see the frontier in their imaginations if not in reality. Travel books exploded from American presses in the decades after independence. Meanwhile, the study of North American geography proved particularly attractive to American intellectuals who believed that they could describe the world in a rational and comprehensive manner. Like constitutions, laws, or medical textbooks, maps could reflect precision and meticulous rationality.[3]

Then there were the seemingly mundane questions that commanded the attention of many Americans. What about Louisiana's soil, natural resources, and climate? Rumors abounded in 1803. With little real evidence to back up his assertions, David Ramsay, who had lectured the people of Charleston on the benefits of the Louisiana Purchase, confidently predicted that "the greatest portion enjoys a salubrious air; and is so fertile, as to be equal to the support of a population, far exceeding the many millions which inhabit Great-Britain, Ireland, France, Spain, and Portugal—I had almost said all Europe."[4]

Other reports were more extravagant. Several newspapers described a great mountain of salt.[5] In a sarcastic take on this and other stories, the *Connecticut Courant* reported "a considerable lake of pure *Whiskey*, which is said very nearly to resemble good old *Irish*

---

[2] Holton, "The Ohio Indians and the Coming of the American Revolution in Virginia," 453-79; McClesky, "Rich Land, Poor Prospects," 449-487; Onuf, *The Origins of the Federal Republic*; Taylor, *Liberty Men and Great Proprietors*, 18-29, 89-101; Taylor, *William Cooper's Town*.

[3] Jackson, *Thomas Jefferson & the Stony Mountain*; Nobles, "Straight Lines and Stability," 9-35. Rueben Gold Thwaites gathered numerous individual accounts during the early part of this century. See Rueben Gold Thwaites, *Early Western Travels*.

Usquebaugh. Should this rumour prove to be well founded, it is believed that most of our newly imported citizens will speedily remove to that country for the sake of securing the free navigation of those *waters.*"[6]

Most of these reports were based on dubious evidence. Although Spanish and British surveyors had created detailed surveys of the Pacific coast, Europeans and Anglo-Americans were at a loss when it came to the continental interior. Early explorers, cartographers, and travelers provided spotty details. Many of the first Europeans to describe the North American interior were themselves committed to its settlement. As a result, they had every reason to exaggerate the environment in ways that would make the region seem more welcoming. When news of the Louisiana Purchase reached the United States, American commentators were only too happy to adopt these fantastic stories for their own purposes.[7]

The administration began to create a portrait of Louisiana in 1803 when Jefferson sent his queries. But the contradictory and uncertain responses made clear that few of the president's contacts had reliable information. So Jefferson dispatched a series of expeditions into Louisiana, ranging from brief excursions to unprecedented, comprehensive journeys.

From 1803 to 1805, the United States attempted to survey the geography and the population of Louisiana through limited travel and ongoing documentary research in Washington. This was a tentative first step toward creating a map of Louisiana. This first period of inquiry was more demographic than scientific or diplomatic. American policymakers simply wanted to know who lived in Louisiana. Jefferson began by asking a Mississippi planter named William Dunbar to survey the Red River Valley. General James Wilkinson also initiated his own efforts. After joining William C.C. Claiborne at the transfer of power in New Orleans, Wilkinson became the first American governor of Upper Louisiana, a position he held without surrendering his appointment as commander of the Army's

---

[4] Ramsay, *An Oration on the Cession of Louisiana to the United States*, 6-8.
[5] *Alexandria [VA] Advertiser*, 30 December 1803; *Connecticut Courant* [Hartford, CT], 7 December 1803; *National Aegis* [Gloucester, MA], 7 December 1803; *Scioto Gazette*, 3 December 1803.
[6] *Connecticut Courant*, 7 December 1803.

western forces. Wilkinson dispatched one of his officers, Lieutenant Zebulon Pike, to explore the upper reaches of the Mississippi River. Meanwhile, other correspondents on the frontier explored their own libraries in an effort to answer the questions that Jefferson posed in his queries. Most of the first "explorers" provided little information on the population, geography, and agriculture in Louisiana. Their reports confirmed that members the administration knew very little about what they had bought from France.

Jefferson quickly responded to these circumstances. From 1804 to 1807, he orchestrated a second period of exploration with more ambitious goals. The most famous of these ventures was the Lewis and Clark expedition, which left St. Louis in the spring of 1804 and reached the Pacific Northwest before returning to St. Louis and then Washington in 1806. Two other teams are less famous now, but were equally important to the administration's attempt to determine exactly what the United States acquired from France. Thomas Freeman and Peter Custis continued the expedition begun by Dunbar, ascending the Red River Valley in the summer of 1806. Finally, Zebulon Pike led a second expedition, this one across the Plains and the eastern Rockies in the winter of 1806-1807.

All three expeditions bore the same Jeffersonian stamp. They combined diplomacy with science. They also forced men to acquire skills that were alien to their own professions. Meriwether Lewis, William Clark, and Zebulon Pike were all professional soldiers who doubled as naturalists for the purposes of their expeditions. Thomas Freeman, an Irish-born surveyor and civil engineer who had helped design the layout for Washington, D.C., and Peter Custis, a Virginia-born physician who began his medical studies in Philadelphia just as Lewis completed a rushed scientific education, had to learn about diplomacy and military affairs before they entered the disputed Texas-Louisiana border region where Spanish and American troops faced one another.[8]

These expeditions explored three distinct regions of Louisiana: the northern Plains, the central Rockies, and the Red River Valley.

---

[7] Allen, "Geographical Knowledge & American Images of the Louisiana Territory."

[8] Flores, *Jefferson & Southwestern Exploration*, 49-54, 59-60. The notes of the Freeman and Custis Expedition were published in a variety of sources soon after its completion. Unlike the Lewis and Clark expedition, however, these books and newspaper articles presented highly abridged and edited narratives. Flores has masterfully compiled the fragmentary journals remaining into a single chronicle of the expedition.

Lewis and Clark, leading the first of the expeditions, took the northern route. As Jefferson explained in his instructions to Lewis and Clark, "The object of your mission is to explore the Missouri River, & such principal stream of it, as, by it's [sic] course and communication with the waters of the Pacific ocean, whether the Columbia, Oregan[sic], Colorado or any other river may offer the most direct & practicable water communication across this continent for the purposes of commerce."[9] Jefferson's goal was to locate the Northwest Passage, a mystical maritime route through North America that Europeans had sought for centuries. He started organizing the expedition in 1802 and indeed composed his instructions before receiving news of the Louisiana Purchase. At the time, the Spanish continued to govern Louisiana, and Spanish officials were logically wary of an American military expedition across their territory. So when Madison attempted to secure passports for Lewis and Clark, the Spanish quickly rejected the application. The Louisiana Purchase removed this diplomatic impediment, however, and by the end of 1803 Lewis and Clark had moved to the banks of the Mississippi for their final preparations. Jefferson immediately dispatched further instructions to Lewis, informing him how best to proceed in the new international conditions.[10] It was during these preparations that Lewis wrote his December 19, 1803, letter to Jefferson informing the president of his preparations.

What followed was a trek that lasted over two years and crossed the western two-thirds of North America. The men of the Lewis and Clark expedition toiled up the Missouri River through the summer and fall of 1804, a demanding physical task against a powerful river. The following year, the expedition traversed the Rocky Mountains before descending the Columbia River to the Pacific Coast. In 1806, Lewis and Clark led a faster return trip, reaching St. Louis in the fall.

Famous though their expedition might be, Lewis and Clark were not alone. Secretary of War Henry Dearborn gave Wilkinson permission to launch an expedition through the southern Plains and

---

[9] Jefferson to Lewis, 20 June 1803, *Letters of the Lewis and Clark Expedition*, I: 61.
[10] Jefferson to Lewis, 16 November 1803, *Letters of the Lewis and Clark Expedition*, I: 136-8.

"THE GRAND EXCURSION"

into the Rockies. Those mountains had long fascinated Americans, and the wild speculation that came in the wake of the Louisiana Purchase included the hope that the Rockies would possess vast mineral deposits. Once again, Wilkinson turned to Zebulon Pike, fresh from his journey to the upper Mississippi. Like the Lewis and Clark expedition, however, Pike's goals were not limited to science. He, too, had diplomatic orders. Like Lewis and Clark, he was to cultivate friendly relations with Indians inhabiting land that the United States now claimed. As Wilkinson instructed Pike, "you are to turn your attention to the accomplishment of a permanent peace," not only between the United States and the Indians, but also among Indians who seemed likely to go to war with each other. During these travels, Pike was also supposed to conduct a general survey of the Plains as well as the Arkansas and Red Rivers.[11]

Thomas Jefferson did not initiate either of Pike's expeditions. These were very much James Wilkinson's endeavors. Wilkinson, confident in his authority to make his own decisions, dispatched Pike to the upper Mississippi without contacting the administration. Yet the similarity between Pike and Lewis and Clark attested to a set of shared objectives that reached beyond Jefferson and extended beyond science. American officials believed that exploring Louisiana would help settle all the uncertainties created by the Louisiana Purchase.

In addition to these similar motivations, the leaders of the two expeditions faced similar dangers. Not only did they worry about an unforgiving climate and potentially hostile Indians, but Pike, like Lewis and Clark, feared Spanish efforts to intercept his expedition. Pike avoided the common trails, instead taking his men through the valleys at the foothills of the Rockies. This was rough, forbidding terrain, but he hoped the route would hide the expedition.

Pike displayed characteristic panache in the midst of peril. Surrounded on all sides by the central Rockies, Pike decided to climb the largest mountain he could see. While the rest of the expedition built a crude shelter, Pike, in company with three other men,

---

[11] Wilkinson to Pike, 1 June 1806, *Journals of Zebulon Pike,*"I: 285. See also Dearborn to Wilkinson, 16 October 1805, Carter, XIII: 10; Jackson, *Thomas Jefferson & the Stony Mountain,* 250.

"marched early, with an expectation of ascending the mountain." He described it in nonchalant terms, expecting to reach the mountaintop in a day. The appearance of the Rockies, he wrote, "can easily be imagined by those who have crossed the Alleghany." This comparison indicated just how much Pike underestimated the size and altitude of the Rockies' peaks. The Rockies put eastern mountain ranges like the Alleghany to shame. In light clothing, their feet covered with slippery leather boots, the trio scrambled up the mountain for two days, struggling for breath in the thin atmosphere. On November 27, Pike "arose hungry, dry, and extremely sore." He abandoned the ascent, stumbling back to the camp where his men waited. He recorded a detailed description of what later became known as Pike's Peak, but Zebulon Pike himself never reached the summit of the mountain that bears his name.[12]

Pike began his expedition in the summer of 1806. His departure coincided with the third American foray into Louisiana. With Lewis and Clark in the North and Pike in the center, Freeman and Custis explored the South. They were to conduct a general survey of the Red River Valley, gathering information on the Lower Mississippi Valley that proved so elusive in 1803. On April 19, 1806, Freeman and Custis left Fort Adams, an outpost on the eastern banks of the Mississippi a short distance above the confluence of the Mississippi and Red Rivers. Creeping northwest, Freeman and Custis' men traveled through land that now constitutes northwestern Louisiana and southwestern Arkansas.

Freeman and Custis found the Red River Valley both beautiful and unpleasant, an avenue for future commerce and a sluggish bottleneck. It looked like a wonderland for American farmers, trappers, and fishermen. Their observations even predicted the future of southern cuisine. Custis found that, "The Pecan continues plenty, along with numerous other nuts, trees, and vegetables."[13] The land seemed extremely fertile. "They are found to be more productive than the best Mississippi lands and the cotton always commands a higher

[12] *Journals of Zebulon Pike*, I: 348-52.
[13] Flores, *Jefferson & Southwestern Exploration*, 115.

price than that of the Mississippi."[14] Freeman added that "cat Fish were taken at the camp near the village, of from 15 to 70 pounds weight, equal in taste and flavor to any caught within the U. States."[15]

Like visitors before and after, Freeman and Custis devoted much of their time to discussing the weather. They were passing through humid, malaria-infested waters at the height of summer. The worst came on July 7, when they sweltered in ninety-six degrees. In August, they often awoke to early mornings in the upper seventies. By the afternoon, it was usually over ninety. The only relief from the blazing heat came in the form of sudden downpours that proved unpleasant in their own right. Their journal monotonously recorded overcast days that often included "excessive rain" or "much rain."[16]

Despite the scientific focus of their journals, Freeman and Custis were well aware of the diplomatic controversy that surrounded their expedition. Their fears were valid. The success or failure of Jefferson's three expeditions turned on both the skills of the explorers and their ability to navigate the contested landscape of the North American interior. That navigation was diplomatic as well as geographic. Lewis and Clark proved to be exceptional cartographers. Not only did they keep meticulous records of their two years of travel, but they rarely took a wrong step. Yet their success was also due in no small part to their skilled negotiations with the Indians of the Plains, the Rockies, and the Pacific Northwest. They avoided or resolved conflicts. Through two long winters—first with the Mandan of modern North Dakota in 1804-1805 and then with the Clatsop during 1805-1806 in the region that now constitutes Oregon and Washington—Lewis and Clark sustained their expedition by establishing good relations with their Indian hosts. Not only did Indians allow them to proceed through the continental interior, but a successful—let alone speedy— transit of North America was highly unlikely without the geographic knowledge that Indians provided.[17]

The winters also provided Indians with periods of intensive negotiation and exploration. The Corps of Discovery presented the

---

[14] Flores, *Jefferson & Southwestern Exploration*, 110.
[15] Flores, *Jefferson & Southwestern Exploration*, 157.
[16] Flores, *Jefferson & Southwestern Exploration*, 336-43.
[17] Ronda, *Lewis and Clark Among the Indians*, 67-12, 181-213.

Indians of the Plains, Rockies, and the Pacific Northwest with their official delegates of the United States government. While Lewis and Clark wrote extensive descriptions of all facets of Indian life, the Indians got only a transitory glimpse of the United States that was both militaristic and gendered. The hierarchical structure of the Corps of Discovery was not an accurate reflection of political or social relations in American civilian life. Meanwhile, the only woman on the expedition was an Indian, Sacagawea. Her relationship with her French-Indian husband, Toussaint Charboneau, would have been familiar to most Indians of North America, many of whom had encountered these interracial unions. But Indians receive no information on the complex rules dictating the codes of behavior for white men and women in the United States. From the Indian perspective, Americans were peculiar travelers and often ungrateful guests who made demands on the Indians for supplies and information.

If Lewis and Clark benefited from their contact with Indians, the fact that they *avoided* contact with other whites was no less important. The Spanish perceived the expedition as part of a broader American campaign to infiltrate Spanish territory and undermine Spain's alliances with Indians. Nor were they incorrect, for Lewis and Clark did indeed exceed even the most generous definitions of the Louisiana Purchase. Though Upper Louisiana was American territory purchased from France, the Spanish owned the territory on the far side of the Rocky Mountains. That the Spanish never found Lewis and Clark enabled the expedition to continue. Other American explorers were not so lucky.

The almost lighthearted title of "The Grand Excursion," which Freeman and Custis used to refer to their expedition, belied the problems of climate and diplomacy they encountered. Diplomatic controversy eventually brought the expedition to a premature end. Spanish troops intercepted the expedition near the Caddo villages. Convinced that the expedition was, in fact, a prelude to future

"THE GRAND EXCURSION"

American incursions into Texas, the Spanish troops forced the Americans to reverse course. The encounter heightened tensions between the United States and Spain, which were only resolved through the creation of the Neutral Ground, the demilitarized buffer zone between Texas and Louisiana.[18]

Like the Indians who encountered the Lewis and Clark expedition, the Caddo also learned from their encounter with Freeman and Custis. They were already familiar with whites. The useful lesson the Caddo received was that tense relations existed between Spain and the United States. They learned to exploit these tensions later.

Pike and his subordinates suffered the worst fate of the three expeditions. They had problems navigating the terrain and encountered insurmountable diplomatic obstacles. Through the winter of 1806-7, chronically short of food and carrying no heavy clothing, Pike's men withstood the Rocky Mountains. Spotting what they took for the Red River Valley, they headed south. The Red River would carry them through the Southwest and join the Mississippi a short distance above New Orleans.[19] Unfortunately they were not descending the Red, but the Rio Grand, going deeper and deeper into Spanish territory. It was only as they approached the Spanish outpost of Santa Fé that Pike ascertained their location. While dispatching Dr. John Robinson, a physician accompanying the expedition, to Santa Fé, his men built a small fort by an isolated riverbank. It was here the Spanish found them.[20]

What followed was a process of indirect negotiation, with strategic concerns often discussed in humanitiarian terms. Robinson told the Spanish of Pike's location, and on February 16 a detachment of troops offered supplies and transportation for Pike's men to leave Spanish territory. Pike refused. Ten days later, American lookouts spotted two Frenchmen, probably fur traders. The Frenchmen informed Pike that Governor Joaquin de Real Alencaster knew of Pike's location. Alencaster cast himself as Pike's defender, claiming that Utah Indians planned an attack on the expedition. Alencaster

---

[18] Flores, *Jefferson & Southwestern Exploration*, 204; Jackson, *Thomas Jefferson and the Stony Mountain*, 230-4; Weber, *The Spanish Frontier in North America*, 254.
[19] Jackson, *Thomas Jefferson & the Stony Mountain*, 253.
[20] *Journals of Zebulon Pike*, I: 374-5.

dispatched fifty soldiers "to protect me, and that they would be here in two days." Pike concluded that the Spanish were looking for more than an opportunity to "protect" the Americans, and "to this I made no reply." Like Freeman and Custis, however, there were few options. Pike mounted his horse and rode a scant twelve miles to the Spanish camp.[21]

What followed was a new expedition into the heart of Spanish Mexico. The Spanish imprisoned Pike's men. They released Pike along with most of his party after a few months, but kept four men for two years. A fifth, Sergeant William Meek, was convicted of killing another expedition member, Private Theodore Miller, and it was thirteen years before he was released.

The outcome of these expeditions highlighted their objectives. Jefferson's scientific goals remain the most intriguing to this day, but Jefferson himself never forgot the diplomatic and commercial purposes for sending men to the frontier. Just as Jefferson believed the rivers of the Ohio and Mississippi Valleys would provide the "principal channels of future commerce," so too did he hope the Red, Missouri, Columbia Rivers would provide similar avenues farther west. And after all the rumors of mountains of salt and lakes of whiskey, Jefferson hoped Pike would establish exactly what resources were available in the Rockies.

Most importantly, however, Jefferson wanted all of these explorers to help him create a map of Louisiana that would settle once and for all what the United States had purchased in 1803. Such a map would provide scientific information, which would satisfy the president's personal interests, and commercial possibilities, which would serve the nation's economic interests. Nonetheless, Jefferson's most immediate concerns remained diplomatic. Scientific and commercial information were useful to the United States, but only if the nation could establish unchallenged sovereignty to a Louisiana Purchase with clear boundaries.

These objectives do not mean that the explorers themselves were not committed scientists. Consider an entry from Freeman's journal.

[21] *Journals of Zebulon Pike*, I: 379-84.

Illustrations (clockwise from top): Charles Wilson Peale, *William Clark* (1810), Independence National Historical Park. Color plate, page 177; Charles Wilson Peale, *Zebulon Pike* (1808), Independence National Historical Park. Color plate, page 181. Charles Wilson Peale, *Meriwether Lewis*, Independence National Historical Park. Color plate, page 178;

He referred to the expedition's leadership as "Thomas Freeman, Surveyor, who was furnished the requisite instruments, for determining Geographical positions, by Astronomical Observation; Dr. Peter Custis whose attentions was directed to Botany, and Natural History."[22] Freeman defined Custis and himself as naturalists. At a time when "scientist" had not entered the public lexicon, Freeman and Custis nonetheless saw themselves as men who devoted themselves to the study of the natural world. The neophytes Lewis and Clark were equally sincere in their scientific pretensions and the samples they gathered set the standard for American botanists. Nonetheless, Lewis and Clark used other words throughout their adult lives to describe their professions. Soldier and, eventually, territorial governor were the most common titles.

It is tempting to trace the lives of these explorers after they returned, searching in their subsequent experiences for some explanation of their success or failure as explorers. Such a biographical focus is fundamentally frustrating, however, because there was no pattern to subsequent events. For example, Meriwether Lewis, the most successful of the explorers, encountered innumerable and eventually overwhelming difficulties in later life. Lieutenant Zebulon Pike, though a poor navigator who became a Spanish prisoner, was promoted when he returned and pursued a successful military career. During the War of 1812, when so many American generals were ineffective, Pike emerged as a talented commander, rising to the rank of brigadier general while still only thirty-four years old.

Rather than look for a pattern through a strict examination of success or failure, the best way to make sense of the explorers is to consider them as products of the frontier. With one notable exception, the leaders and many of the subordinates on Jefferson's three expeditions all chose to stay on the frontier. Freeman became a surveyor and land commissioner. Lewis and Clark became territorial governors. Pike continued to serve with the army at various frontier

---

[22] Flores, *Jefferson & Southwestern Exploration*, 100.

"THE GRAND EXCURSION"

encampments. A number of the men who traveled with Lewis and Clark—the group about which historians have the most information—met rough ends, often in violent encounters with Indians. Still others settled permanently with Indians. Only Peter Custis, the most sophisticated scientist to journey west, abandoned the frontier altogether, choosing instead the more settled life of a physician in North Carolina.[23]

The map that Jefferson and Madison sought was a long time coming. Newspapers and private publishers were quick enough to run accounts of the expeditions, but they often relied on dubious sources. In 1814, after years of delay, William Clark finally published a map of western North America. Meriwether Lewis and Zebulon Pike were already dead, the victims of suicide and battle in the War of 1812, respectively. In preparing the map, Clark drew mostly from his own observations, but he also used information gathered by George Drouillard, who had accompanied Lewis and Clark, Dunbar, Freeman, Pike, James Wilkinson, Jr., the general's son who traveled with Pike, and older maps by European cartographers. He also borrowed from more recent mapmaking ventures of the men who founded Astoria, a Columbia River fur-trading post that constituted the first American entrepreneurial endeavor on a continental scale.

Publication of Clark's map coincided with the release of the first book-length account of the Lewis and Clark expedition. The book and the map told separate stories. The book chronicled the adventures of a single expedition as it crossed the Plains and the Pacific Northwest. Clark's map was more expansive, bringing together the work of various expeditions and explorers. It coalesced a brief period of exploration and encounter that covered the continent. It was a synthesis of the personal struggles American explorers faced as they rowed and marched through the West. It also put centuries of Indian observations into print.[24]

[23] Flores, *Jefferson & Southwestern Exploration*, 308-14; Clarke, *The Men of the Lewis and Clark Expedition*, 37-61.
[24] Jackson, *Thomas Jefferson & the Stony Mountain*, 272-80.

Illustration: William Clark, *A Map of Lewis and Clark's Track* (1814), courtesy of the Library of Congress. Color plate, page 179.

Clark's map was, in fact, what so many Americans wanted in 1803. It made sense of Louisiana and helped satisfy the craving to understand what Americans had acquired through the Louisiana Purchase. The map combined exacting cartography with superb artwork. But Clark considered the details of mountains and rivers more important than a record of the populations that filled the North American interior. The only references to the residents of North America—whether Indians or European settlers—were a few indications of where Indian tribes tended to congregate. There were no portraits of Indian villages, commercial routes, or white settlements. As a result, Clark's map belied some difficult realities: the American landscape was spotted with numerous settlements, populated by people with a bewildering mix of ancestries.

Clark's omissions were reasonable. After all, his mandate was to provide a record of the natural geography. By the time that map was published, however, Clark had already spent years helping to build a stable government in the West for those very people he had left out of his map. Clark knew as well as anybody that governing the West would prove as difficult as exploring it.

Chapter Ten
The Expanding Nation

William Clark worried so much about the people in Louisiana because he was forced to contend with so many tasks. As a militia commander and Indian agent, he traveled throughout the eastern prairie, visiting isolated white settlements and Indian villages. Later, as territorial governor, he wielded power from an office so simple it would have embarrassed the governor of an eastern state. In every context, he feared that the government of the United States might not be able to provide for white citizens, control African-American slaves, or establish its sovereignty over Indians.

Nor was Clark alone in his concerns. Americans worried a lot about Louisiana. To European observers, this anxiety no doubt seemed strange, for American expansion seemed unimpressive to European powers that had acquired colonies throughout the globe on a scale that dwarfed the Louisiana Purchase. But Americans were convinced that the very attitude of the Europeans was part of the problem. Many Americans had concluded that the European habit of building large empires was corrupt to its core. This attitude was, of course, the result of the experiences many Americans had as colonists themselves. When Britain, France, and Spain created their American empires, for example, they assumed that colonies should be subservient to the mother country. Americans rejected this subservience out of hand, and it was the British attitude of superiority that led men like Jefferson and Madison to seek independence. Americans were predisposed to reject jurisdictional inequality of the sort practiced by Europeans. Then there was the text of the Louisiana Purchase itself, which guaranteed that the residents would enjoy "all these rights, advantages and immunities of citizens of the United States." So inequality was neither palatable nor possible in the wake of the Louisiana Purchase.

These conditions left a perplexing problem: what would become of the people and land acquired through the Louisiana Purchase? Would Louisiana become a colony of America? The experience of the colonial era told Jefferson and Madison that Louisiana had to become a full member of the American nation. They looked to American independence for some options. Americans had to construct new governments on the frontier soon after the thirteen colonies gained their independence. By the time the United States acquired Louisiana, Americans had more than two decades experience organizing the western frontier. Even the most optimistic Americans marveled at the growth they saw in the West. For example, the population of Kentucky, the first new state in the West, grew from 73,677 people in 1790 to 220,955 in 1800. The rapid growth of white population on the northwestern frontier led Congress to create the state of Ohio only months before receiving news of the Louisiana Purchase.

This story should sound familiar. The tremendous migration of Americans into the western territories led federal officials to see threats to American sovereignty if foreign nations controlled the Mississippi River. Western migration also transformed the way Americans thought about their government, convincing them that the United States needed a government on the scale that many Americans had rejected in 1776. Americans agreed that settlers would wither on the vine without an administrative structure to govern them, an economic system to maintain prosperity, and a military to defend them.[1] Public officials also worried that chaos and violence might spread throughout the West. George Washington himself believed that "instead of adding strength to the Union," disconnected and unhappy western settlers would become "a formidable and dangerous neighbour."[2] Americans forged a consensus that no state was capable of administering the West. The federal government was best equipped to shoulder the burden.

[1] Cayton, *The Frontier Republic*; Aron, *How the West was Lost*.
[2] George Washington to Henry Knox, 5 December 1784, quoted in Onuf, *Statehood and Union*, 4. See also Banning, *The Sacred Fire of Liberty*, 255-8; Slaughter, *The Whiskey Rebellion*.

Americans looked on expansion as a timeless challenge faced by every empire since the Romans. They were wary because they believed that empires had never been able to expand without eventually disintegrating. The American solution to this ancient problem was the territorial system. Their first assumption was that large territories were too unwieldy to govern. So the first task was to divide the land into manageable portions that could eventually become states. The model they used was that of a family, and the relationship between the government and the territories was that of parent to children. The federal government would protect, instruct, and guide the territories during their formative years. Once the territories proved their maturity, they could become states equal to their neighbors, independent on many local matters while still loyal to the American family.[3]

The territorial system was a radical idea and marked a clear break from the European imperial systems that had dominated the Americas. American territories would not exist simply to serve the older settlements. Americans instead reversed this system, arguing that the federal government would serve the territories, protecting them and welcoming them into the union.

By 1803 the territorial system seemed to be working. The frontier was stable and prosperous. The new states of Kentucky, Tennessee, and Ohio had already entered the union. Other territories like Indiana and Mississippi were developing at a rapid pace. The children of the new nation were being schooled in its principles. When they were ready, when they had built institutions of a civil society, when their populations had grown and stabilized, territories could become states.

It was in this context that the United States bought Louisiana, and Americans scrambled to graft the territorial system onto their new western domain. Congress began by dividing the land. Lower Louisiana became the Territory of Orleans. Upper Louisiana entered a more nebulous status. Renamed the District of Louisiana, it fell under the jurisdiction of the Indiana Territory. In 1805, under pressure from

---

[3] Onuf, *Statehood and Union*, 44-87.

the residents of Louisiana, Congress amended the governance plan to give Orleans an elected territorial house of representatives separate from the District of Louisiana. Congress renamed the District of Louisiana, creating the Territory of Louisiana.[4]

As was the case in all new territories, there were few elected offices in either the Territory of Orleans or the Territory of Louisiana. Both territories eventually received an elected house of representatives, but all other public officials—including governors, judges, and local officials—were nominated by the president and approved by the Senate. The secretary of state had final authority over territorial policy, but the numerous State Department appointees constituted the bulk of the civil government along with numerous other officials serving the Treasury and War Departments. The federal government assumed its paternal role until the Louisianians were ready to govern themselves. As New York Congressman Samuel Mitchill explained, the residents of Louisiana would "serve an apprenticeship to liberty...they are to be taught the lessons of freedom; and by degrees they are to be raised to the enjoyment and practice of independence." In other words, these people would learn to be Americans.[5]

The "apprenticeship to liberty" lasted the better part of a decade in the Territory of Orleans and almost twice as long in the Territory of Louisiana. Becoming a new state was not a simple process. In addition to proving they knew how to participate in representative government, the residents of Louisiana also had to complete a rite of passage. They had to craft a state constitution. This document would do more than provide a government. Territorial residents had to prove they knew how to govern themselves in a manner consistent with the principles of a free society.

Congress did not consider statehood for the Territories of Orleans and Louisiana until 1811 and 1818, respectively. On April 30, 1812, nine years to the day after the date on the Louisiana Purchase, Louisiana became the eighteenth state. The Louisianians chose an

---

[4] *Statutes at Large*, II: 322-3, 331-2.
[5] *Annals of Congress*, XIII (Eighth Congress), 480.

equally symbolic date for their first election. On July 4, 1812, the voters of Louisiana went to the polls to select state officials. Not to be outdone by their neighbors to the south, in 1812 the residents of the Territory of Louisiana argued in a painfully mixed metaphor that the "sister territories of Orleans, Mississippi and Indiana, are fast approaching to political manhood."[6] Congress responded by renaming the section surrounding St. Louis the Missouri Territory to avoid any confusion with the new state of Louisiana. Creating an elected territorial house of representatives and forming a compact territory shaped like other western states was an obvious step in the direction of statehood. And by the end of the decade, the Missourians had sufficiently proven their "political manhood" that Congress created the State of Missouri in 1821.[7]

But what would these governments do? After all, governments in the early nineteenth century had only a fraction of the power that the state and federal governments wield today. Perhaps so, but from a nineteenth-century perspective, the western territories of the United States were home to a vast, complex, expensive federal bureaucracy. Every territorial official from governor to coroner was a federal appointee. The Louisiana Purchase caused a tremendous increase in the number of men on the federal payroll. Add to this the fact that almost half the United States Army was stationed in Louisiana, and the result was a federal force numbering in the thousands.

The men who governed Louisiana faced innumerable tasks. In addition to assuming the responsibilities that would normally belong to a state government, they faced additional burdens that were particular to resolving the Louisiana Purchase. They had to distribute millions of acres of land, whether by upholding old colonial land grants or by creating new grants under American rules. Determining who owned the land also meant establishing a new legal system. In the Lower Mississippi Valley, that meant combining the American common law with the complicated Franco-Spanish law that had emerged under colonial rule. In Upper Louisiana, the absence of an

---

[6] Letter to the editor, 17 August 1811, in *"Louisiana Gazette,* 3 October 1811.
[7] For documents leading up to the change in government, see Petition to Congress from the Inhabitants of the Territory of Louisiana, 9 September 1811, Carter, XIV: 471-2; Resolutions of a Meeting of the Town and District of St. Louis, 5 November 1811, Carter, XIV: 484-5.

established legal tradition—or, for that matter, a large community of lawyers—meant that local residents had to build a legal system from scratch.[8]

The territorial government also had to establish its control over Louisiana's non-white residents. The militia in the Territory of Orleans spent much of its time patrolling for slaves, hunting for runaways and locating suspected revolts. When the militia and the New Orleans City Guard, a precursor to the city's police force, failed to capture runaway slaves, Louisianians complained in 1810 that "the delinquents go bold by impunity and lose every respect and every fear of the magistrates."[9] Meanwhile, the large contingent from the United States Army serving in the Territory of Louisiana was hard at work preventing Indians from opposing white settlement west of the Mississippi.

The governors who served in the Territories of Orleans and Louisiana tell a great deal about the kind of system that Jefferson, Madison, and Monroe hoped to create in the land acquired through the Louisiana Purchase. Their successes, frustrations, and failures attested to the numerous agendas at play on the western frontier.

The most consistent fixture in this process was William C.C. Claiborne, who served as governor of the Territory of Orleans during its nine-year existence. Claiborne was only twenty-eight years old when he arrived in New Orleans. A Virginia native, he moved to Tennessee in 1794, where he served first as a judge and later as a Congressman. It was in Tennessee that Claiborne met Eliza W. Lewis of Nashville. The two married in 1801. Later that same year, Jefferson selected him to serve as the governor of the Mississippi Territory. The Claibornes had a sentimental attachment to Tennessee, and they named their one child Cornelia Tennessee.[10]

Claiborne's proximity to Louisiana and his experience on the frontier made him a logical if not self-evident choice to take charge of Orleans. Like James Monroe, Claiborne could be remarkably thin-skinned. He was petty, often self-pitying, and once became so enraged by a political opponent that he injured the man in a duel, suffering a

---

[8] Dargo, *Jefferson's Louisiana;* Banner, "The Political Function of the Commons."
[9] *Proceedings of the Conseil de Ville,* V: 232. For additional comments on the City Guard, see *Proceedings of the Conseil de Ville,* II: 107, VI: 1-2, V: 182, VI: 169, VIII: 247, X: 48-50
[10] Hatfield, *William Claiborne,* 3, 20-1, 94-108.

serious bullet wound himself. But he was a loyal Republican familiar with frontier government, and, although a man of modest talent, he proved an extremely capable governor. One observer explained that Claiborne "is a *good sort of man* and tells a number of good *long* stories," a backhanded compliment that actually testified to the diffuse mixture of political beliefs, management skills, and experience that, together, led the administration to define a successful governor.[11]

When Claiborne reached Louisiana, his expectations had not changed since he wrote his letter to Madison from Natchez in September 1803. He was confident "Republicanism has many professed admirers here," but added, "I fear that Republicanism among all her friends here will find but a few who have cultivated an acquaintance with her principles."[12] He concluded that a long time would pass before the local residents became good American citizens. "I am inclined to an opinion," he wrote to Jefferson, "that until a *knowledge* of the American Constitution, Laws, Language and customs, is more generally diffused, a State Government in Louisiana, would not be managed with discretion."[13]

Claiborne described wholesale corruption among public officials as well as a listless white population that lived off the labor of potentially dangerous black slaves. He was hardly alone in these opinions. Many believed Louisiana would be impossible to govern. When Isaac Briggs arrived in New Orleans in 1804, for example, he informed Jefferson that the government of colonial Louisiana "has been very corrupt...Despotism and Licentiousness have been equally conspicuous." He believed that "considerable time is necessary to change, radically, long established habits."[14]

Claiborne faced the tasks of governing a large population consisting mostly of white settlers and black slaves, all jammed into a small area. The Territory of Orleans seemed crowded to visitors from the rest of the United States, with the busy streets of New Orleans and the plantations heading off in all directions. Upper Louisiana was a different story. Larger and more sparsely populated, its residents were

---

[11] David Porter to Samuel Hambleton, 18 July 1810, *David Dixon Porter Papers*, Library of Congress Manuscript Collection, Book 1; Prichard, "Selecting a Governor for the Territory of Orleans," 269-393.

[12] Claiborne to Madison, 2 January 1804, *Madison Papers*, Reel 8. For similar examples, see Claiborne to Madison, 10 January 1804, *Madison Papers*, Reel 8; Claiborne to Madison, 1 January 1804, *Madison Papers*, Reel 8; Claiborne to

scattered and often on the move. Most white residents worked as trappers, traders, or other occupations that required constant movement. While many of the Indians lived in permanent villages, their contact with whites was nonetheless more sporadic than in the crowded Lower Mississippi Valley. American policymakers were well aware of these differences. It therefore followed that governing Upper Louisiana and Lower Louisiana followed different rules and timetables.

There was no political figure to match Claiborne's importance or his tenure in office. The men and women who passed through Upper Louisiana were more transient, and their leaders were no different. Territorial leaders came and went, and that sense of change was itself indicative of life in Upper Louisiana. Three of them—James Wilkinson, Meriwether Lewis, and William Clark—offer an instructive lesson in the legacy of the Louisiana Purchase.

When Congress created the Territory of Louisiana in 1805, Jefferson selected Brigadier General James Wilkinson, the senior officer in the United States Army and immediate commander of the nation's western forces, to serve as governor. Trained as a physician, Wilkinson abandoned medicine to fight in the American Revolution. A military career agreed with him, and Wilkinson rose quickly through the officer corps, spending most of his career fighting Indians in the West. In 1803, he was at the summit of the nation's military pyramid, often describing himself as the heir to George Washington, a citizen soldier who wanted nothing more than to defend the nation.

But Wilkinson was no George Washington and everybody around him knew it. Nonetheless, members of the administration concluded that, despite his limitations, Wilkinson had proven effective in a series of western commands. He seemed a logical choice to take charge of the new Territory of Louisiana. As he offered Wilkinson the governorship, Jefferson flattered him as a person "Reposing special Trust and Confidence in [Wilkinson's] Patriotism, Integrity, and Abilities,".[15]

Madison, 31 January 1804, *Madison Papers*, Reel 8. Claiborne presented a less negative, but nonetheless uncertain view of the potential of the residents of New Orleans in a letter to Secretary of War Henry Dearborn, 31 January 1804, *Claiborne Letterbooks*, I: 356-7; Claiborne to Madison, 13 February 1804, *Madison Papers*, Reel 8.

[13] Claiborne to Thomas Jefferson, 29 September 1803, *Jefferson Papers*, Reel 47.

THE EXPANDING NATION

Jefferson had good reason to believe Wilkinson would make a capable governor. The general was used to life on the frontier and his army career provided plenty of experience organizing large numbers of men far from the nation's center. But Wilkinson encountered trouble from the moment he arrived. Political factions were already forming in St. Louis, and by attempting to play one side against the other, Wilkinson converted civil disagreements into vicious partisan battles. The governor seemed well on his way to creating exactly the sort of disagreement in the West that Jefferson had hoped to avoid.[16]

Unknown to the president, Wilkinson was, in fact, on the Spanish payroll. Moving to St. Louis only made the situation easier for Wilkinson, providing easy access to Spanish officials in Texas and making Wilkinson seem all the more important to the Spanish, who were eager to know about American intentions in Louisiana. Despite his duplicity, Wilkinson remained an eager servant of the United States. He was apparently able to accommodate both his loyalty to the United States and his service to the Spanish. He reached St. Louis keen on building an orderly government. Like Claiborne to the South, Wilkinson predicted a difficult job, but expressed every confidence that he could both preserve American sovereignty and establish an American government in the Territory of Louisiana.

Within a year, Jefferson was forced to defend Wilkinson against rising criticism. "Not a single fact has appeared, which occasions me to doubt that I could have made a fitter appointment than Genl Wilkinson," Jefferson informed his secretary of the navy, Robert Smith, in 1806.[17] Still, Wilkinson seemed incapable of promoting a stable political climate. More concerned with the general's competence than his loyalty, Jefferson ordered Wilkinson to resume direct command of the troops stationed in the Southwest. It seemed an easy way to remove Wilkinson from St. Louis without the controversy of removing him from office.

Clever though it might be, dispatching Wilkinson from St. Louis did not get Jefferson any closer to building an American government

---

[14] Isaac Briggs to Jefferson, 2 January 1804, Carter, IX: 146-8.

[15] Jefferson to Wilkinson, 11 March 1805, *Jefferson Papers*, Reel 52; Wilkinson to Madison, 7 April 1805, Carter, XIII: 114-5.

[16] Wray, "The Administration of General James Wilkinson"; Foley, *The Genesis of Missouri*, 159-82.

[17] Jefferson to Robert Smith, 4 May 1806, Ford, VIII: 450.

in the Territory of Louisiana. His experience with Wilkinson taught him that only trustworthy men should serve as territorial governors. So in February 1807 Jefferson chose Meriwether Lewis. In the months following Lewis' return from the expedition, Jefferson had searched for a way to reward the explorer. Lewis had shown leadership, intelligence, good management, diplomatic skills, and a remarkable talent for improvisation at moments of crisis. Who better to serve as governor in the Territory of Louisiana?

Choosing Lewis made sense to the President, but so had the selection of Wilkinson two years before. It soon became apparent that Jefferson had made a serious error in selecting Lewis. Lewis encountered problems that overwhelmed his considerable energies. Most of these were Lewis' fault. He took more than a year to assume office and remained aloof from his neighbors. More importantly, however, Lewis, like Wilkinson, was unable to realize either the political or economic goals crucial to establishing a peaceful order in the Territory of Louisiana. The complexities of territorial trade eluded Lewis, and he soon faced criticism from local merchants as well as his own business partners. St. Louis residents also squabbled with one another in a way that generated feuds rather than stable political dialogue. While Claiborne's administration in the Territory of Orleans was marked by activity, reform, and success, the situation in Louisiana seemed to have calcified.[18]

Jefferson would forgive Lewis for almost everything and protect him. Lewis could make no similar claim to the patronage of President James Madison, who assumed office soon after Lewis arrived in St. Louis. Nor could he expect much support from Robert Smith, who left the Navy Department to become Madison's secretary of state. Neither Madison nor Smith had any close personal friendship with Lewis. Besides, Madison soon concluded that Smith was both disloyal and incompetent, and the ensuing conflict between them left territorial governors to fend for themselves. Lewis came under constant criticism from other territorial officials and local residents. The most pointed

---

[18] Ambrose, *Undaunted Courage*, 435-49; Foley, *The Genesis of Missouri*, 213-4.

THE EXPANDING NATION

attacks came from Frederick Bates, the territorial secretary and Lewis' immediate subordinate. He explained "the unpopularity of the governor" this way: "he has brought in on himself with harsh and mistaken measures. He is inflexible in error." Lewis became convinced that critics in Washington were attacking his conduct and his character. Bates had little sympathy. In a letter to his brother, Bates referred to Lewis as "a big baby."[19]

A crisis arose in the summer of 1809 when Secretary of War William Eustis asked Lewis to explain alleged financial irregularities. Lewis wanted to respond to the criticism in person. He left St. Louis for Washington, explaining, "All I wish is a full and fair Investigation."[20] He followed the lengthy overland route that took him through Tennessee. On the evening of October 11, 1809, Lewis and his secretary, James Neely, were searching for a place to spend the night near Chickasaw Bluff, Tennessee. Lewis went on ahead, and when Neely caught up, he learned that a woman at a nearby farmhouse had discovered:

> Lewis to be deranged...the woman reports that about three oClock She heard two pistols fire off in the Governors Room...he had shot himself in the head with one pistol, & a little below the breast with the other—when his Servant came in he says; I have done the business my good Servant give me Some water. he gave him water, he Survived but a short time.[21]

It fell to another explorer to gather the modest possessions of Meriwether Lewis. Thomas Freeman was serving as a surveyor in the Territory of Louisiana. The meticulous and dispassionate quality of Freeman's record of the Red River Expedition three years before was evident in the more somber task of gathering Lewis' belongings. He cataloged objects ranging from "One Cambrick handkerchief" to "One [bundle] Maps & Charts."[22]

The death of Meriwether Lewis has always posed difficult questions. Some people have raised the intriguing possibility that Lewis was murdered. The surviving evidence does not support this

---

[19] Frederick Bates, in Marshall, *The Life and Papers of Frederick Bates*, 64.
[20] Lewis to Eustis, 18 August 1809, Carter, XIV: 290-91.
[21] James Neely to Jefferson, 18 October 1809, *Jefferson Papers*, Reel 73.
[22] Thomas Freeman, Memorandum of Lewis' Personal Effects, 23 November 1809, Jackson, ed., *Letters of the Lewis and Clark Expedition*, II: 470-1; Flores, *Jefferson & Southwestern Exploration*, 314.

conclusion, but eliminating that theory still gets historians no closer to a satisfying answer for an obvious question. Why would somebody who could withstand the danger and privation of a cross-country expedition kill himself because of personal criticism? A more fundamental question is how could someone who had been such an effective explorer in Louisiana prove to be such an unsuccessful governor?

The answer to the second question provides a good deal of insight into the first. For all his talents, Meriwether Lewis was ill prepared for the realities that awaited him in the Territory of Louisiana. His youth and inexperience, which some biographers have emphasized, do not account for the problems he encountered in St. Louis. After all, Lewis was thirty-four when he arrived in St. Louis, six years *older* than Claiborne when Claiborne became governor of Orleans. No, age alone cannot explain the fate of Meriwether Lewis. Instead, Jefferson's process of selecting a governor proved to be fundamentally flawed. This was true for James Wilkinson as well as Meriwether Lewis. Jefferson incorrectly assumed that military leaders could serve as civil administrators. Successful though he was at leading a small team of military volunteers, Lewis—like Wilkinson—could not master the complexities of government. Both men were unable to satisfy the disparate interests of western settlers. They were unable to build a political system that promoted the amicable resolution of local disputes. Jefferson sometimes relied too heavily on unquestioned loyalty to republican principles and the Republican party instead of the administrative skills, the tact, or the savvy needed to manage Louisiana.

Even after death, Lewis remained subject to attack. Although people lamented his death, white residents of the Territory of Louisiana complained about ongoing commercial disputes resulting from Lewis' policies. Neighboring Indians also complained. A lieutenant in the United States Army, Eli B. Clemson, reported in March 1810: "the Osage Indians Appear to be much dissatisfied in

Consequence of a treaty that was made by Governor Lewis in 1808."[23]

If talents and shortcomings explain the differences between the Lewis and Clark Expedition and Lewis' tenure as governor, then the possibility of disgrace explains why Lewis was incapable of responding to his collapsing fortunes. At a time when most public figures saw no distinction between their public reputation and their private dignity, personal disgrace could prove too much to bear. Those notions of reputation go a long way toward explaining Lewis' suicide.[24]

At the time, the death of Meriwether Lewis did not generate much attention. Only in later years would Americans study the subject in depth. Not only did federal leaders have few questions about his death—they were convinced it was suicide—but an answer got them no closer to building a stable American regime. In the years that followed, a series of men executed the powers of governor of the Territory of Louisiana.[25] Almost a decade after James Wilkinson took charge, Madison finally identified a man who could master the considerable responsibilities of a territorial governor. There was a certain poetic justice when the president nominated William Clark governor in 1813. The succession served as a reminder of the close friendship that made Lewis and Clark such an effective team both during and after the exploration of Louisiana. Clark had returned to Louisiana with Lewis, beginning his tenure as commander of the territorial militia and director of territorial Indian policy.

Unlike Lewis, Clark understood the connections between politics and government, commerce and economics, diplomacy and warfare. He rapidly acquired a reputation in Washington as a talented frontier official. During the War of 1812, he helped organize an effective defense against both British invasion and Indian war. Clark occasionally mismanaged domestic politics and sometimes stimulated tensions between white settlers and Indians, but, under his leadership, the territorial government was at least stable. Federal policymakers in Washington also never doubted that Clark would

---

[23] Eli Clemson to Eustis, 28 March 1810, Carter, XIV: 399.
[24] Freeman, "Dueling as Politics;" Freeman, "Slander, Poison, Whispers, and Fame." The death of Meriwether Lewis remains a subject of fascination. For various interpretations, see Ambrose, *Undaunted Courage*, 465-74; Kushner, "The Suicide of Meriwether Lewis."
[25] John Wayles Eppes to Madison, 8 February 1810, *PJM-PS2*, 21; Madison to Benjamin Howard, 18 April 1810, Carter, XIV: 403-4; *Biographical Directory of the American Congress*, 112.

attempt to implement their policies. This reliability was particularly welcome compared to the situation further east, where some state governors seemed incapable of implementing the administration's priorities at best and actively opposed wartime strategy at worst. Like policymakers in Washington, Clark believed commerce was just as important as good government for binding together the people of the Territory of Louisiana. Clark focused particular attention on the fur trade as an effective means to connect people throughout the West. As governor he continued the work he and Lewis started when they negotiated with Indians during their expedition across the continent.[26] Clark became the federal government's point man in the difficult process of building commercial networks throughout Upper Louisiana.

William Clark spent six years as territorial governor. Despite his successes, however, he was unable to build a powerful electoral coalition. When Missouri became a state in 1821, he recognized that he could not win election as governor with the ease he had secured appointment as a territorial governor. William Clark continued to serve the United States government as he had his entire adult life, through federal patronage rather than through election. He assumed the post of surveyor general for Missouri, Illinois, and the newly created Arkansas Territory. Experienced, reliable men like him were all the more important to federal leaders as white settlers moved west of the Mississippi during the 1810's and '20's. Congress responded by further dividing the land acquired through the Louisiana Purchase. The Territories of Arkansas, Iowa, and Minnesota soon joined Louisiana and Missouri to create an unbroken line of American governments running the length of the Mississippi Valley.

Unlike Clark, William C.C. Claiborne made a smooth transition to state politics. In 1812 he became the first governor of the State of Louisiana, even defeating Francophone opponents despite the fact that Creoles and French migrants remained the majority of the population. The state's constitution limited Claiborne to a single term, and in 1816 he began to think of a return to the East. In 1817 the same coalition

---

[26] Cox, "A World Together, A World Apart," 112-47; Jones, *License for Empire*, 1-20; Prucha, *American Indian Policy in the Formative Years.*

that helped Claiborne win the governor's race helped him secure the legislature's selection as senator (although some states eliminated this practice later in the nineteenth century, all U.S. Senators were not elected by popular vote until 1913). After thirteen years in Louisiana, Claiborne took several months in 1817 to settle his affairs and say his good-byes. Perhaps he waited too long. On the eve of his departure for Washington, Claiborne suddenly fell ill. On November 17, 1817, the *Louisiana Courier* published a brief announcement stating, "Died last night, at half past eight o'clock, the honorable WILLIAM CHARLES COLE CLAIBORNE...His funeral will proceed from the Government House this day at 4 o'clock P.M." Doctors referred to a "liver ailment," a vague term they employed in the absence of a more definite cause of death.[27]

Claiborne and Clark became more successful territorial governors than Wilkinson and Lewis because they knew how to build political coalitions within the territories they governed. Clark's political organization was not sufficient to secure an electoral majority for governor, but it was enough for a successful reign as territorial governor. Claiborne and Clark, like Jefferson and Madison, recognized that they had to build inroads with the Louisianians. William Clark may have created a map that made Louisiana seem vacant, but he knew as well as anybody that Louisiana was anything but an empty landscape. It was instead a crowded frontier filled with people struggling to adapt to the changes wrought by the Louisiana Purchase.

---

[27] *Louisiana Courier*, 17 November 1817.

Chapter Eleven
"An Apprenticeship to Liberty"

While presidents and cabinet members, congressmen and senators created governments in Louisiana, one fear guided their thinking. If they failed to create a stable system that satisfied the residents of Louisiana, those same residents might attempt to create independent republics or, worse, they might invite European powers to return to the Mississippi Valley. The prospect of domestic resentment seemed just as likely—and just as dangerous—as the foreign intervention that Americans hoped to prevent by settling Louisiana's borders. Those fears emanated from a single question that people on both sides of the Mississippi began to ask. What would the Louisiana Purchase mean to the residents of Louisiana?

An indication of this question's importance became clear on December 20, 1803, when the French government surrendered Lower Louisiana to the United States. Representatives of three nations—Pierre Clément Laussat (the French Prefect), the Marquis de Casa Calvo (until a few weeks before the Spanish governor), and Claiborne and Wilkinson (the American commissioners)—presided over a public ceremony in which power changed hands. The location was the Place d' Armes, the square that served as the political, economic, and social hub of New Orleans.[1]

Rumors about the transfer soon drifted throughout the United States. Some stories told of people weeping as the French flag descended and the flag of the United States took its place. But were they tears of sorrow or tears of joy? Some Americans predicted years of resistance from the local population. Others were more optimistic, concluding that the tears were proof of the Louisianians' joy at

---

[1] Claiborne to Madison, 20 December 1803, *Claiborne Letterbooks*, I: 306-9; Daniel Clark to Madison, 1 January 1804, *Consular Dispatches*, New Orleans.

"AN APPRENTICESHIP TO LIBERTY"

Illustration: The transfer of Louisiana from France to the United States, Thure De Thulstrup, Louisiana Historical Society. Image courtesy of the Louisiana State Museum. Color plate, page 180.

becoming American citizens. As is so often the case, both interpretations contained grains of truth. Few residents resisted the cession of Louisiana to the United States. At the same time, they often objected to the terms imposed on them by Americans. People in Louisiana shared a desire to take charge of their political destinies, but some found that their definitions of what it meant to be an American collided with that of their neighbors.

Although his presence at the Place des Armes on December 20 cannot be confirmed, Jacques Villeré probably watched the proceedings. Thirty-five years after his father had died following the 1768 revolt, Villeré was a senior militia officer. Most likely Villeré paraded alongside other local troops during the handover. Villeré was well aware of the importance of this moment. For the third time in his life, distant leaders had transferred Louisiana. Like many Louisianians, he believed joining the United States could deliver tremendous benefits. Nonetheless, he knew from personal experience what could happen when newcomers took charge. Along with his fellow Louisianians, Villeré studied the Americans very closely.

The first signs were not good. Villeré and other white Louisianians watched as the United States attempted to superimpose the territorial system onto Louisiana. They took offense at the absence of elected offices, which smacked of colonialism. In 1804 residents of both the Territory of Orleans and the District of Louisiana sent a blistering report to Washington explaining, "we knew that it was impossible to be citizens of the United States without enjoying a personal freedom, protection for property, and, above all, the privileges of a free, representative Government." Louisianians asked troubling questions. "Are truths, then, so well founded, so universally acknowledged, inapplicable only to us?" they asked. "Do political axioms on the Atlantic become problems when transferred to the shores of the Mississippi?"[2]

White Louisianians made clear from the beginning that far from resenting the Louisiana Purchase, they resented any plan that

---

[2] Remonstrance of the People of Louisiana Against the Political System Adopted by Congress for Them," in *ASP: Miscellaneous*, I: 396. The Remonstrance focused on broad constitutional questions. Three months later, another memorial, this one emphasizing legal and administrative questions, arrived from the Louisiana District. See *ASP-Miscellaneous*, I: 400-5.

"AN APPRENTICESHIP TO LIBERTY"

distinguished them from other Americans. White Louisianians set out to convince their new fellow countrymen that they were eager to join the American national community. In 1810, for example, the Territorial House of Representatives in Orleans informed Congress, "The inhabitants of the territory of Orleans, become your Country men by a Combination of political events, but are satisfied with the title of Citizens of the United States, as they had acquired it from choice." In this and other public statements, white Louisianians asserted their loyalty to both the United States and to republican government.[3]

White Louisianians had various reasons for welcoming the Louisiana Purchase. They agreed with Jacques Pitot and Berquin-Duvallon that Louisiana had suffered under French and Spanish colonial rule. By contrast, they predicted that membership in the United States could bring unprecedented prosperity. They hoped to gain access to trade routes, to investment capital, and to new slaves. Men in Louisiana also wanted greater political freedoms, which they associated with the United States and which seemed so different in European colonies. They were particularly eager for statehood, when they would be able to vote for their leaders and, equally important, seek high public offices themselves.

So the Louisianians remained loyal, nobody more so than Jacques Villeré. In the years that followed he advocated strong ties between white Louisianians and the Americans. He also continued to rise in the territorial and state governments, eventually commanding the state militia during the War of 1812. When the British prepared to invade the Gulf Coast, Villeré and other white Louisianians like him faced the most direct test of their loyalty. The British were convinced that white Louisianians were "Unconnected by blood or long fellowships with the other States of America" and predicted that "there can be no doubt but a considerable party might be formed in favor of a separation from the United States."[4] In the summer of 1814, the British even dispatched a pamphletto "Spaniards, Frenchmen, Italians and British...in Louisiana." They claimed that "the american

---

[3] Orleans House of Representatives to Congress, 12 March 1810, Carter, IX: 873. See also Resolution of the Orleans Territorial Legislature, 20 February 1807, Carter, IX: 707; Orleans House of Representatives to Thomas Jefferson, 19 January 1810, *Jefferson Papers*, 74.
[4] James Sterling Memorandum, 17 March 1813, HNO.

usurpation in this country, must be abolished."[5]

Ignoring these appeals, Villeré remained steadfast in his belief that American citizenship brought unchallenged benefits to white Louisianians. Most of his fellow white Louisianians agreed. The Louisiana militia provided crucial support to the federal troops under Andrew Jackson, helping create one of the worst defeats for the British army.

In the wake of the Battle of New Orleans, Andrew Jackson thanked the Louisianians for their sacrifices. "I shall soon leave you, my fellow-citizens," Jackson said in March 1815. He called on Louisianians to "defend your constitution and your country, as you have done, against all open attacks in war." He also congratulated Louisianians for their help in defeating the British.[6] In the following years, Louisianians made certain that Americans did not forget their service in the War of 1812. Hardly a public celebration or a private party went by without some statement or toast reminding people how the Louisianians had helped turn back the invasion.

These actions had the desired effect. Many Americans came to believe that, though Louisiana and Missouri might seem strange, they were nonetheless home to loyal citizens and republican government. American territorial officials soon proved to be the Louisianians' most fervent allies. When Louisianians began mobilizing for statehood, Claiborne informed an influential Louisianian named Julien Poydras, "I am sincerely friendly to the proposed Change." He wrote of the prospect of statehood, "My support of this measure...[proceeds] from an impression that it will be attended with great national benefits."[7] William Clark did the same, endorsing the appeal for statehood without once questioning the loyalty or the political maturity of the Louisianians.

Claiborne proved to be particularly enthusiastic in his celebration of the Louisianians. His letter to Poydras reflected a growing friendship between the two men. Although Claiborne often

---

[5] Edward Nichols Broadside, 29 August 1814, *Edward Nicholls and William H. Percy Letters*, HNO, Folder 1.
[6] Andrew Jackson to the citizens and soldiers of New Orleans, 31 March 1815, *Papers of Andrew Jackson*, III: 337.
[7] Claiborne to Julien Poydras, 2 September 1811, *Claiborne Letterbooks*, V: 351. See also Claiborne to Poydras, 18 July 1811, *Claiborne Letterbooks*, V: 307-8; Claiborne to Albert Gallatin, 18 August 1811, Carter, IX: 944-5.

"AN APPRENTICESHIP TO LIBERTY"

wrote of the Louisianians as politically naïve, he believed they were nonetheless inclined toward republican government. Meanwhile, Louisianians warmed to Claiborne, expressing their support in the most tangible form during Claiborne's successful bid to become the state's first governor in 1812. His closest challenger was Villeré. Villeré accepted the defeat, returned to his plantation, and welcomed his commission as a general in the state militia. Rather than resent Americans like Claiborne, he had long ago learned the necessity of accommodation. Villeré set out to build his own political constituency within the American community.[8]

Villeré was not alone, nor were the connections between Louisianians and Americans limited to the political world. Louisianians and Americans began to marry one another, and few families attested to this better than the Claibornes, the Duraldes, and the Clays. Both Eliza and Cornelia Claiborne, William C.C. Claiborne's wife and daughter, respectively, died of yellow fever only months after crossing the Mississippi. In 1806, Claiborne married a Creole named Clarissa Duralde, and they soon had a son named William Charles Cole, II. Meanwhile, Clarissa's brother, Martin Duralde, married Susan Hart Clay, the daughter of Congressman Henry Clay. Finally, Clarissa and Martin Duralde's sister, Julie, married Henry Clay's *brother*, John Clay, an attorney who had settled in New Orleans. Gatherings of the Duralde family must have been confusing to say the least. Family connections this complicated were few and far between, but the fact that Louisianians and Americans could form happy families proved to many people that the broader American nation could count on Louisiana as one of its family.[9]

Claiborne's marriage to Clarissa was brief. In November 1809, three years after they were married, Clarissa became ill. For years Claiborne wrote a series of letters to Washington describing the minutia of life in the Lower Mississippi Valley. Late November and early December 1809 are striking for the *absence* of outgoing correspondence. Claiborne broke his silence on December 17. In a

---

[8] *Journal of the House of Representatives of the State of Louisiana* (New Orleans, 1812), 14.
[9] For the rise of the Duralde family and its connections with the Clays and Claiborne, see Claiborne and Thomas Bolling Robertson to David Porter, 6 May 1809, *Claiborne Letterbooks*, IV: 349; Claiborne to Martin Duralde, Seth Lewis, and Thomas Oliver, 31 May 1811, *William C.C. Claiborne Papers*, LSU; Clay to Caesar A. Rodney, 17 August 1811, *The Papers of Henry Clay*, I: 574-5.

brief note to Madison, then only six months into his presidency, Claiborne informed Madison that "on the 29th of last month, it pleased Almighty God to take from me my beloved wife...a greater calamity, could not have befallen me.— She was in the Bloom of life...her Smiles relieved anxiety & Sweetened every care. —I am not conscious Sir, of unbecoming weakness; but this misfortune has nearly undone me."[10]

William Claiborne married for a third time in 1812, this time to another Creole, Susanna Bosque, who was less than half his age. She came from a wealthy and prominent Creole family. The reason for the marriage became clear a few months later, when Susanna gave birth to a daughter, Sophronia. A son, Charles, was also born during Claiborne's tenure as governor.[11] When Claiborne's term expired in 1816, a variety of candidates emerged, all of whom claimed to represent the state's best interests. Many had served in the territorial and state legislature. Some were judges or lawyers. The citizens of Louisiana went to the polls on July 4, 1816, and chose a war hero. When the results came in during the weeks following the election, Jacques Philippe Villeré learned that he would be the second governor of Louisiana.[12]

It was a moment of immense satisfaction for Villeré. When he was sworn into office on December 17, 1816, the new governor admitted, "the lively emotions with which I am penetrated deprive me of the power of expressing my sentiments."[13] Almost a half-century after his father had died to establish power for local residents, the Louisianians had chosen one of their own as leader. Villeré was among those who lamented Claiborne's death almost a year later. He celebrated Claiborne in January 1818 as "one of our citizens the most distinguished for his virtues and talents, as well as for the services which he had rendered to the country."[14] The following year Villeré proclaimed Louisiana a firm member of the "great American family," its population delivered from the "idle prejudices between citizens of different origins."[15]

---

[10] Claiborne to Madison, 17 December 1809, Carter, IX: 859.
[11] DeGrummond, "Cayetana Susana Bosque y Fanqui," 277-94.
[12] Courier de la Louisiane, 17 June, 1 June, and 5 July 1816.
[13] Romero, "My Fellow Citizens," 33.
[14] Jacques Philippe Villeré to the Louisiana State Legislature, 6 January 1818, Journal of the House of Representatives of the State of Louisiana (New Orleans: J.C. de St. Romes, 1818), 6.

"AN APPRENTICESHIP TO LIBERTY"

So if white Louisianians were so keen to be Americans, why did they remain the objects of suspicion? Part of the answer is rather simple: it can be difficult to overcome first impressions. Americans assumed Louisianians would resent having their nationality transformed. But there was less benign prejudice at work. The men who governed the United States were almost all Protestants of British ancestry, and they harbored deep-seated resentment toward Catholics. They believed the corruption of French and Spanish colonial governments had only exacerbated the harm done by Catholicism.

The changing political geography of Louisiana meant that Louisianians endured the same doubts and resentments facing new immigrants to the United States. But Louisianians faced even greater doubts. They seemed more dangerous because they constituted the majority on a tenuous frontier. Worse still, they had not undergone the formal process of naturalization that was supposed to teach foreigners how to be loyal Americans. When Samuel Mitchill spoke of an "Apprenticeship to Liberty," he claimed the territorial system would double as a system of naturalization for America's newest citizens.

Other Americans were even less generous when it came to white Louisianians. Virginia Representative Daniel Sheffey stated, "While he looked upon these people as equals, and was disposed to do them justice, he thought all they could demand at his hands was to be placed on the equality to which they were entitled."[16] It was only through the unflagging loyalty of the Louisianians during the territorial period that American policymakers began to change their minds. When the Territory of Orleans applied for statehood, for example, Congressman Nathaniel Macon borrowed from Samuel Mitchill's statement, claiming the Louisianians "had already served a sufficient apprenticeship to the United States."[17]

White Louisianians also benefited from the fact that they looked particularly loyal in comparison to other residents of Louisiana. American leaders soon suspected that a greater threat came not from white Louisianians, but from slaves, Indians, and even from

---

[15] Villeré to the Louisiana State Legislature, 6 January 1819, *Journal of the House of Representatives* (1819), 5.

[16] *Annals of Congress*, Eleventh Congress, 2nd Session, 484.

[17] *Annals of Congress*, Eleventh Congress, 2nd Session, 485. See also *Annals of Congress*, Eleventh Congress, 2nd Session, 493-507.

Americans. The fear of slaves and Indians predated the Louisiana Purchase and continued unabated. But it was the prospect of a strange separatist conspiracy in Louisiana that took many by surprise. All the more surprising was the leader of that expedition, a man new to the frontier.

The trouble started in 1804 when President Jefferson decided to replace his vice president, Aaron Burr. Jefferson had neither forgotten nor forgiven Burr for challenging him in the election of 1800. By the time Jefferson ran for a second term, the twelfth amendment to the Constitution was in place, allowing presidential candidates to choose running mates. Jefferson selected a different New Yorker, Governor George Clinton, a man who would deliver northern votes and who seemed far more reliable than Burr.

Even before the election of 1804, it was clear that Aaron Burr had been banished from the Republican leadership in Washington. Burr was no more popular in New York, where he lost a bid for governor in 1804. Then, in July 1804, Burr killed Alexander Hamilton in a duel that outraged even Hamilton's enemies. At the age of forty-eight Burr's political prospects—both in Washington and in New York—were finished. Courts in New York and New Jersey issued warrants for his arrest. In less than a year, Burr went from vice president to wanted criminal.

So Aaron Burr looked west. Historians have struggled to isolate exactly what he intended to do. Unfortunately, neither Burr nor his alleged conspirators left enough evidence to give a clear indication of their intentions. In the absence of a smoking gun, historians depended on the observations of his contemporaries. Officials in Washington and commentators throughout the nation believed that Burr intended to create a separate republic in the Southwest by combining land from Spanish Texas and the Territory of Orleans. What made this so horrifying to many Americans was the thought that their fellow countrymen might just succumb to Burr's ranting.[18]

---

[18] Abernethy, *The Burr Conspiracy;* McCaleb, *The Aaron Burr Conspiracy;* Crackel, *Mr. Jefferson's Army,* 113-6, 130-52. Scholars have investigated the Burr Conspiracy for decades. The search has always been a frustrating one. There are few incriminating documents, no real smoking gun, and plenty of letters that conflict one another. Instead, historians have always depended on accusations that were later leveled against Burr and Wilkinson. But the fears of Americans occasionally had little to do with actual events. Many Americans had feared for years that

"AN APPRENTICESHIP TO LIBERTY"

Whatever Burr was planning, he believed he had an ally in James Wilkinson, then serving as governor of the Territory of Louisiana. But the same unpredictability that made people in Washington wary of Wilkinson now undid Aaron Burr. Wilkinson probably recognized that Burr had only limited public support. He also knew that federal leaders would use whatever force necessary to suppress separatist schemes. At the critical moment in the winter of 1806-1807, Wilkinson rejected Burr and became an occasionally overzealous instrument of the government policy to root out all Burr sympathizers in the Southwest. On November 25, 1806, he provided a deposition explaining that he had only pretended to form an alliance with Burr in order to gather information. One contact promised Wilkinson that Burr "had proceeded too far to retreat." Once he knew the details of the conspiracy, Wilkinson explained that he "became indifferent about further disguise." He joined the chorus of people warning the president of his former colleague and in the process distanced himself from the conspiracy.[19]

Wilkinson's instincts proved accurate. Jefferson dispatched federal troops who scoured the West and eventually dragged Burr back to Virginia for trial. Chief Justice John Marshall presided over the court, and many Americans awaited news of Burr's conviction for treason.[20] The government's evidence was weak. Prosecutors provided evidence that Burr had formed some kind of organization, but they presented no conclusive proof that the goal of that association was treasonous. Burr was acquitted. The verdict was small consolation to Burr, who settled in Europe. When Aaron Burr returned the United States in 1812, he was a defeated man who struggled to resurrect both his fortune and his reputation until his death in 1836.[21]

Throughout the crisis of 1806-1807, what proved most striking was the absence of support for Aaron Burr within Louisiana itself. White Louisianians made certain to remind Congress of that fact. They dispatched memorials to Congress calling conspicuous attention to "our unshaken fidelity in the midst of treasons and conspiracies,

---

western states and territories would be fertile ground for separatist schemes. When Burr disappeared into the West, these people–including Jefferson, Madison, and many members of Congress–immediately suspected the worst. The best record of Burr as well as the most detailed analysis of his activities is to be found in the second of a two-volume collection of his writings. See Kline, *Political Correspondence and Public Papers of Aaron Burr.* The editorial note in volume II, 1006-8 provides a succinct discussion of the administration's response to Burr.

Illustrations (left to right): John Vanderlyn, *Aaron Burr* (1809), New York Historical Society. Color plate, page 182; Charles Wilson Peale, *James Wilkinson*, Independence National Historical Park. Color plate, page 181.

are irrefagible proofs of the incorruptibility of our honor and of the sincerity of our affection to our common Country." This statement, and others like it, did more than provide a barometer of public of opinion in Louisiana. It also showed how politically sophisticated frontier residents could be. Whatever white Louisianians might believe, they recognized that condemning Burr provided the ideal opportunity to prove their own loyalty.[22]

White Louisianians benefited by contrasting their own loyalty to that of Americans like Burr. They were even more successful convincing the American government they shared a common interest in controlling Indians, slaves, and free people of color. Indians, slaves, and free people of color in turn asked the same question facing white Louisianians: what would the Louisiana Purchase mean for them? They compared what they knew about the United States to their own experiences under European rule. The fundamental brutality of slavery was the same regardless of regime, but slaves and free people

---

[19] Wilkinson Deposition, 25 November 1806, *Annals of Congress*, XVI (9th Congress), 1007-8.
[20] Hay to Jefferson, 14 June 1807, *Jefferson Papers*, Reel 62; Hay to Jefferson, 1 June 1807, *Jefferson Papers*, Reel 62.
[21] Jefferson to Hay, 26 May 1807, *Jefferson Papers*, Reel 62; Peterson, *Thomas Jefferson and the New Nation*, 870-4.
[22] Orleans House of Representatives to Congress, 12 March 1809, Carter, IX: 874.

"AN APPRENTICESHIP TO LIBERTY"

of color had enjoyed opportunities in French and Spanish Louisiana that were unprecedented in the United States. Slaves had more avenues to freedom. These legal differences help account for the large population of free people of color, who, in turn, secured a degree of prosperity unequaled in the United States, let alone the slave-owning South.[23]

Free people of color could not vote, hold office, or engage in certain forms of commerce. At the same time, they did create opportunities unparalleled in the rest of the United States. Free men of color had social and economic links with white Louisianians. Free men of color had their own militia, a fact all the more striking in a United States where laws usually prohibited African-Americans from owning firearms, let alone parading with them in uniform. At a time when miscegenation was a crime in many southern states, white men and black women had open affairs.[24]

Free people of color initially had high hopes for the Louisiana Purchase. In 1804 a group of free men of color wrote to Congress, "We are Natives of this Province and our dearest Interests are connected with its welfare. We therefore feel a lively Joy that the Sovereignty of our Country is at length united with that of the American Republic." The absence of any reference to race in the Louisiana Purchase opened the possibility that they, too, might become citizens of the United States. "We are duly sensible that our personal and political freedom is thereby assured to us for ever, and we are also impressed with the fullest confidence in the Justice and Liberality of the Government towards every Class of Citizens which they have here taken under their Protection."[25]

American leaders would sorely disappoint free people of color. The three men who orchestrated the Louisiana Purchase—Jefferson, Madison, and Monroe—all claimed to oppose slavery, but they recoiled at the prospect of a large population of free people of color. They were incapable of accepting the principle of equal status for people of African ancestry. Like many white Americans, they assumed

---

[23] "The Law of Slavery in Spanish Luisiana," in Haas, ed., 51-70; Hall, *Africans in Colonial Louisiana*, 304-6; Hanger, *Bounded Lives, Bounded Places: Free Black Society in Colonial New Orleans, 1769-1803*.

[24] McConnell, *Negro Troops of Antebellum Louisiana: A History of the Battalion of Free Men of Color* (Baton Rouge: Louisiana State University Press, 1968), 3-32.

[25] Address from the Free People of Color, January 1804, Carter, IX: 174.

that free people of color might lead slave revolts. After all, free people of color led the revolution in Saint-Domingue. Americans in Washington and in the territorial regime set out to impose new legal restrictions on slaves as well as free people of color. White Louisianians were only too willing to go along with these restrictions, for many of them feared a slave revolt and resented the competition they faced from free people of color.[26]

The 1806 Black Code in the Territory of Orleans put things bluntly. The law stated, "As the person of a slave belongs to his master, no slave posses any thing in his own right, or dispose in a way of the product of his industry, without the consent of his master."[27] The Black Code continued, "Free people of color ought never to insult or strike white people, nor presume to conceive themselves equal to the white; but on the contrary that they ought to yield to them in every occasion, and never speak or answer to them but with respect, under the penalty of imprisonment according to the nature of the offense."[28] Free people of color were prohibited from cavorting with slaves, which whites assumed would inevitably lead to racial revolt. For years many white Louisianians had sought restrictions like these. This was especially true of plantation owners who were surrounded by their own slaves. It took the arrival of American government and American views on race and slavery to bring that new system into being.

Slaves responded in kind. They ran away in increasing numbers, hoping to secure their freedom by disappearing into the borderlands between western Orleans and East Texas.[29] Even in their worst nightmares, however, whites could not know what was coming. On January 11, 1811, a massive slave revolt exploded on the banks of the Mississippi just above New Orleans. Within twenty-four hours, over two hundred slaves were marching on New Orleans. They were apparently intent on forcing the territorial government to accept a restructured racial regime. The revolt was all the more striking for the organization that slaves brought to the endeavor. They formed

---

[26] Jefferson, "Amendment to the Constitution," contained in undated memorandum from 1803, *Jefferson Papers*, Reel 47.
[27] Martin, *A General Digest*, 616.
[28] Martin, *A General Digest*, 640-2.
[29] Nemecio Salcedo y Salcedo to Claiborne, 2 January 1808, *Claiborne Letterbooks*, IV: 164-5; Claiborne to Madison, 1 January 1809, *Territorial Papers*, Reel 10.

military companies and some white observers even reported seeing uniforms and flags.[30]

White residents demanded protection. One newspaper soon reported, "The mischief done is not ascertained—there is, however, reason to apprehend that several of our fellow citizens have been masacred, some dwelling houses burnt and others pillaged."[31] As General Wade Hampton, Wilkinson's replacement as commander of troops in the Southwest, observed, "the confusion was great beyond description." He was talking as much about white Louisianians as African Americans, for the revolt caused panic throughout New Orleans and the surrounding area.[32]

Hampton had no qualms about what to do. He was a South Carolina planter who owned numerous slaves, and he dispatched his own troops together with Louisiana militiamen to attack the slaves. A brief and vicious battle followed on January 11, 1811. Despite the slaves' numerical superiority, it was a one-sided contest. Armed with knives and farm implements, the slaves attacked soldiers equipped with muskets and swords. By the end of the day the field was strewn with dead and wounded slaves. The rest sought safety in the countryside.[33] One observer, Peter Ogden, characterized the situation in appropriate terms. He referred to "the war" between free people and slaves in Louisiana. The victor of the war was slavery.[34]

Twenty-nine slaves were captured, including a slave named Charles whom many whites suspected of leading the revolt. In an impromptu trial held, appropriately enough, on a plantation, a three-man panel sentenced Charles to death along with twenty others.[35] Samuel Hambleton, the U.S. naval agent in New Orleans, described the grisly aftermath. The convicted slaves, he wrote, "were hung for the sake of their heads, which decorate our levee...They look like crows sitting on long poles—Charls[sic] had his hands chopped off, then shot in one thigh and then in the other, until they were both broken—Then shot in the body and before he was expired was put into a bundle of straw and roasted!"[36]

---

[30] Claiborne to Smith, 7 January 1811, *Claiborne Letterbooks*, V: 95-6; Claiborne to Smith, 9 January 1811, *Claiborne Letterbooks*, V: 95-6; Dormon, "The Persistent Specter," 394; Aptheker, *American Negro Slave Revolts*, 19-51; Gayarré, *History of Louisiana*, IV: 266-8; Ingersoll, "Free Blacks in a Slave Society," 198.

[31] *Louisiana Gazette*, 11 January 1811.

[32] Wade Hampton to Eustis, 11 January 1811, Carter, IX: 917.

The 1811 uprising may well have been the largest slave revolt in U.S. history. Whites swore it would never happen again, passing more restrictions on slaves. Despite the assistance of the free black militia in putting down the revolt, whites remained convinced that free people of color had helped foment the violence. Although there was no subsequent insurrection to match the 1811 revolt, slaves continued to seek their own freedom by running away. During the British invasion of 1814-1815, for example, African-Americans found safety with the enemies of the United States. Jacques Villeré dispatched his militiamen to hunt down runway slaves. A planter himself, Villeré was deathly afraid of losing his own human property. Two weeks after American forces defeated the British, Villeré wrote personally to General John Lambert, the British commander, condemning his officers for deciding to "kidnap" Louisiana slaves. He even sent a bill for $450 in damages to his own plantation.[37]

While the chasm between slavery and freedom often determined the way white, black, and mixed-race Louisianians responded to the Louisiana Purchase, geography usually determined Indian reactions. Indians took a pragmatic approach to the Purchase, meeting with varying degrees of success. They faced whites, who moved onto Indian land and then demanded the United States government protect them in the face of the violent Indian reprisals. William Clark found himself in the unenviable position of mediating these disagreements. As an explorer and then as head of Indian affairs, he had proven more sympathetic to Indians than other whites. As territorial governor, however, his primary responsibility was to white settlers. In 1815, for example, he reported, "eight parties of hostile Indians...have visited the frontiers of this Territory and killed *ten* men. One of these parties (a few days ago) attacked a small french Village...they killed 4 men plundered the houses and burnt down part of the town." In the same letter he expressed his own pleasure that the War Department had dispatched a force of 500 troops to the Missouri Territory "as a Check to the Indians."[38]

---

[33] Dormon, "The Persistent Specter," 394.
[34] Peter Ogden to Nathaniel Evans, 11 January 1811, *Evans Papers*, I, 14-5
[35] "Summary of Trial Proceedings," 470-1.
[36] Samuel Hambleton to David Porter, 25 January 1811, *David Dixon Porter Papers*, LC, Book 2.
[37] Villeré to John Lambert, 29 January 1815, *Jacques Philippe Villeré Papers*, HNO, Folder 63.

"AN APPRENTICESHIP TO LIBERTY"

Resolution eluded William Clark in large part because Indians refused to become subservient children to the Americans. Like other American officials, Clark failed to appreciate that Indians recognized the pitfalls of economic dependence on the United States. They knew what had happened in the East, where white domination led to Indian suffering. In the long run, Clark had to choose whether he would serve Indians calling on the United States to honor its treaty agreements or protect white settlers. There was never really a choice. Like other civil and military officials, Clark's primary responsibility was the welfare of white settlers. Although Clark was committed to a just system on the frontier, he saw no reason to break from the system he had always known.

Clark was also surrounded by other officials who might respect the power of individual Indians but saw no reason to let Indians dominate disputes. In 1819, for example, George Sibley, one of the government's official trading agents with the Indians, met with two Iowa chiefs named Hard Heart and the Crane. "I have desired them to refrain from interfering with the surveyors now at work in the Country they claim," Sibley informed Clark, arguing that it was not for Indians to determine land ownership.[39]

John C. Calhoun, who served as James Monroe's secretary of war, expressed the attitude of many Americans. "The indians must be made to yield the exercise of their barbarous custom..to the milder influence of our laws," he informed Indian Agent John Jamison in 1818.[40] To Calhoun, it was not sufficient for the Indians to acknowledge American sovereignty over the Louisiana Purchase. They had to accept American laws and practices.

The Caddo were the first to suffer. The Transcontinental Treaty, the source of so much happiness for American officials, spelled disaster for the Caddo. With the Neutral Ground eliminated by a permanent boundary of the Louisiana Purchase, the Caddo lost their bargaining power. The federal government finally forced the Caddo "to yield to the milder influence of our laws." The Caddos' experience

---

[38] Clark to the Secretary of War, 17 April 1815, Carter, XV: 25.
[39] George Sibley to Clark, 3 February 1819, Carter, XV: 515.
[40] John C. Calhoun to John Jamison, 8 January 1818,ÄThe Papers of John C. Calhoun, III: 476. For similar comments, see Jamison to Calhoun, 26 May 1819, Papers of John C. Calhoun, IV: 75-6; Jamison to Calhoun, 16 June 1819, Papers of John C. Calhoun, IV: 110; Calhoun to Jamison, 5 July 1819, Papers of John C. Calhoun, IV: 149-52.

was indicative of what befell other Indians on the Eastern Plains. The government's role in that process only served notice that western settlers were in fact far *more* dependent on the federal government than their countrymen in the East. The army removed Indians, creating new possibilities for white settlement. Federal land commissioners established the legal claims that formed the bedrock of land redistribution. Congress authorized a vast web of postal routes that connected westerners to the rest of the nation.[41]

The end of the Neutral Ground came in 1821, the same year that Missouri became a state. Taken together, the two events signaled the completion of the Louisiana Purchase. The United States absorbed the *land* it acquired through the Louisiana Purchase. Establishing federal authority over the Indians was indicative of the effort by the United States to absorb the *people* of Louisiana.

To the Caddo, the Louisiana Purchase created a brief moment of diplomatic advantage. In the long run, however, American possession of the land west of the Mississippi created untold misery for the Caddo as well as for other Indians of the North American West. White Louisianians, on the other hand, reveled in the new political and commercial opportunities awaiting them as citizens of the United States, claiming the Louisiana Purchase was the best thing that ever happened to Louisiana.

---

[41] John, *Spreading the News*, 46-7; White, *"It's Your Misfortune and None of My Own,"* 57-9.

CHAPTER TWELVE
DEPARTURES

William Clark and Dehahuit both died in 1838. Clark had retired in comfort to his adopted home of St. Louis. Dehahuit had opposed the governments of Mexico, the United States, and the independent republic of Texas as they attempted to eject the Caddo from the land they had occupied for centuries. Both men had become fixtures in Louisiana, even as the frontier they knew died. The uncertainty that defined frontiers gave way to clear forms of power. State and federal governments now controlled life in the Mississippi Valley. The contact between Indians, Europeans, and Africans that had been so common during the eighteenth century was replaced by stricter rules and new barriers. Although some people continued to see Louisiana as a land of opportunity, others concluded that the time of possibilities had ended.

In 1820, the State of Louisiana and the Territory of Missouri were home to 153,407 and 66,586 people, respectively. Ten years later, those numbers had risen to an astonishing 240,455 and 215,529. These numbers speak volumes, indicating a wholesale transformation in Louisiana. These changes coincided with the departure—through retirement and through death—of the men who had proven so crucial to shaping the Louisiana Purchase.

One of the first men to leave was Jacques Philippe Villeré. English-speaking American newcomers to Louisiana soon outnumbered the old French-speaking population. This migration in the 1820's would undo the dreams of Villeré, who like many white Louisianians had tried to promote amity between Louisianians and Americans. Villeré watched as the two communities argued with increasing anger. By the time Villeré died in 1830, Creoles, immigrants, and American migrants were all engaged in fierce political battles.[1]

The influx of white settlers also altered the lives of African Americans and Indians. White settlers used slaves in growing numbers. Plantations with hundreds of slaves followed the twists and turns of the Mississippi River in the rich soil of Louisiana. Bumper crops of sugar and cotton fueled Louisiana's economy. While Arkansas and Missouri never became plantation societies on the scale of Louisiana, slavery, nonetheless, flourished there and throughout the Mid-Mississippi Valley. As the number of white settlers and African-American slaves grew, so did the land hunger of whites. White settlers began to move onto land the United States government had promised to Indians. When push came to shove, the federal government—in particular the United States Army—would defend the interests of white settlers before it would respect agreements with Indians.

The transformation of the population west of the Mississippi coincided with a broader change in attitude throughout the United States during the 1820's and '30's. The Napoleonic War in Europe was a distant memory. The boundaries of Louisiana were established. The Spanish empire disintegrated into a series of independent republics. And Americans no longer saw the foreign threats they had feared only a few years before. A generation of Americans had constantly debated foreign relations, but now few Americans considered foreign policy a pressing concern.[2]

Even the style of politics underwent a revolution in the 1820's. The Federalist party had long since collapsed, and now the victorious Republicans were suffering from internal disagreements. A new system of rough-and-tumble politics began to replace the system that produced Jefferson, Madison, and Monroe. Gone was the old distance that separated representatives from their constituents. Voters demanded and sought candidates who would more directly reflect their priorities and their circumstances. The Jeffersonian Republicans

[1] Tregle, *Louisiana in the Age of Jackson*, 79-97.
[2] Lewis, *The American Union and the Problem of Neighborhood*, 199-205.

DEPARTURES

had defeated the Federalists by appealing to these democratic principles. Nonetheless, Jefferson, Madison, and Monroe were hardly men of the people in their private lives or their campaign styles. The three Virginians were ambivalent toward this more democratic political structure because they feared that excessive democracy could lead to chaos.[3]

Andrew Jackson felt no such hesitancy. He proved the master of the new political system. As the old Jeffersonian coalition collapsed, Jackson built a new political organization. Initially referred to simply as "The Democracy," and later the "Democratic Party," Jackson and his followers initiated a new political era much as Thomas Jefferson did a generation before.

The Jacksonians built a coalition that traversed region and reached into the largest cities as well as the rural countryside. But nowhere was Jacksonian politics more popular than in the states and territories carved from the Louisiana Purchase. Western settlers contributed to the changing *style* of American politics as the new democratic politics dominated the national landscape. Those same western settlers also changed in the *substance* of American politics, unleashing new political disputes that commanded the national agenda.

Missouri began this process. Creating state governments west of the Mississippi—a process Jefferson and Madison considered so important to completing the Louisiana Purchase—provided no end of controversy. In 1819 a balance between the number of free and slave states enabled politicians to avoid the issue of the expansion of slavery. With both sides secure in the knowledge that neither interest commanded a clear majority in Congress, they focused attention on other matters. Missouri's appeal for statehood upset that balance. It forced Americans to recognize that numerous territories west of the Mississippi would eventually appeal for statehood, which would only accentuate the debate over whether the expansion of slavery should stop with Missouri.

---

[3] Cayton, *The Frontier Republic*, 39; Taylor, "'The Art of Hook & Snivey'"; Wood, *The Radicalism of the American Revolution*, 262-91.

Members of Congress defused the immediate crisis in Missouri with the unlikely assistance of some unruly characters from Massachusetts. Settlers in the rough northeastern corner of Massachusetts also wanted their own state. They presented a pressure valve to release the tension created by the Missouri Crisis. In 1820 members of Congress agreed to create the free state of Maine in order to counterbalance the slave state of Missouri. American politicians would attempt to preserve this delicate balance by isolating slavery to the South.[4] The Compromise of 1820 offered a temporary solution. As William Clark left office as territorial governor, the Missouri Compromise was only the latest indication of a changing world. The political world he had known—where the tensions between East and West dominated the national agenda—was giving way to a conflict over slavery dividing North from South.

Watching from the sidelines, the generation of the American Revolution seemed mystified and more than a little concerned. Thomas Jefferson lamented the dispute over the extension of slavery. By the time he died on July 4, 1826, at his home at Monticello—fifty years after the Continental Congress finalized the Declaration of Independence—Jefferson considered disagreements over slavery the greatest threat to the union. Try as he might to foster compromise among his fellow citizens, Jefferson freed only eight of his more than 200 slaves, providing the clearest proof that few slaveholders would accept an end to human bondage.[5]

James Madison had a similar reaction from his own plantation, Montpelier, where he had retired in 1817. Like Jefferson, Madison objected to slavery, but he was never able to make the leap to the notion of a truly free or equal society. He rarely condemned the way slaves suffered. Instead, he became most upset about slavery when the issue threatened to cause upheaval among the nation's white population. While Jefferson detached himself from public affairs, Madison attempted to wield influence from retirement. But he had no solution to offer when it came to slavery, nor could he accommodate

---

[4] Moore, *The Missouri Controversy*; Peterson, *The Great Triumvirate*, 49, 59-63; Shoemaker, *Missouri's Struggle for Statehood 1804-1821*, 290-320; Taylor, *Liberty Men and Great Proprietors*, 228-49.
[5] Paul Finkelman, "Jefferson and Slavery: 'Treason Against the Hopes of the World,'" 181-221; Wood, "The Trials and Tribulations of Thomas Jefferson," 410-2.

himself to Jacksonian politics. By the time he died in 1836, Madison was mystified by the world his successors had wrought.[6]

As Madison continued his political fights into the late 1820's, James Monroe retreated from public affairs. In a brief span Monroe suffered personal sadness, financial woe, and increasing physical decline. Monroe, like Jefferson and Madison, proved to be more effective at politics than personal finances. He was deeply in debt in 1830 when his wife, Eliza, died. Monroe soon moved to New York City, where he lived with his daughter and son-in-law. By the end of the year, his own health was so bad that he could not leave his room. What followed were a series of earnest but grim letters to old friends, written with the certainty that it would be the last time Monroe communicated with them.[7] Monroe died on July 4, 1831. His death came fifty-five years after American independence.

To his last days, Monroe continued to defend his actions as a diplomat and as president. Like Jefferson and Madison, he claimed victories during his administration, and selected his own successor. When Monroe had retired in 1825, he followed the precedent of Jefferson and Madison by surrendering power to his secretary of state.

John Quincy Adams was the last of the Jeffersonian presidents. For all his talents, Adams endured a frustrating tenure in which his policies enjoyed little popularity with the American public and his administration faced continual opposition in Congress. The first president to serve only one term since his own father had lost to Jefferson, Adams suffered a humiliating defeat to Andrew Jackson in 1828. The defeat was telling. Adams had helped negotiate the Transcontinental Treaty, which settled the Louisiana Purchase once and for all. That treaty had served the needs of western settlers, but Adams himself never quite grasped the concerns of western settlers. Nor was he able to understand the politics of those settlers. Although four months younger than Jackson, John Quincy Adams was closer in outlook to the older generation of Jefferson, Madison, and Monroe. Even more averse to democratic politics than his predecessors, Adams

---

[6] Banning, *The Sacred Fire of Liberty*, 173-7; Paul Finkelman, "Slavery and the Constitutional Convention: making a Covenant with Death," 188-225; McCoy, *Last of the Fathers*, 253-322.
[7] Ammon, *James Monroe*, 568-73.

was out of step with many of his countrymen.

In contrast to the affluent, Boston-born Adams, Andrew Jackson was a product of the frontier, born to a family of struggling settlers in western South Carolina. He eventually settled in Tennessee. Despite the wealth and influence Jackson eventually accumulated, he never lost touch with what mattered to western settlers, nor did he forget how to communicate with them. As president, Jackson attempted to establish once and for all that Louisiana would be the home of white settlers. Jackson, a wealthy planter in his own right, was a staunch supporter of slaveowners, and he defended settlers who wanted to extend slavery into the new western territories. With overwhelming support from white settlers, Congress passed the Removal Act of 1830 designed to eject Indians still living east of the Mississippi. Jackson eagerly extended the principle of the Removal Act to clear all Indians from areas of white settlement on either side of the river.

In some ways, the Removal Act was only an extension of what the United States had done for a half-century. The Federal government had a consistent record of breaking treaties with Indians. But the provisions of the Removal Act constituted a change. Jackson abandoned the pretext of negotiation, instead stating once and for all that Indians either had to move to land whites did not want or face destruction at the hands of the United States Army. Despite his early attempts at fairness in dealing with Indians, even William Clark endorsed the Removal Act. Clark sensed that settlers and Indians were at odds, and he was unable to promote policies that would curtail the opportunities that white settlers found on the western frontier.[8]

One of the few public voices of opposition to Jackson's policies was John Quincy Adams. Unlike all predecessors, Adams did not believe the end of his presidency meant retirement from politics. He returned to Washington in 1831 as a Congressman from Massachusetts. Adams had remained silent on the issue of slavery while serving the Jeffersonians. In the 1830's he emerged as a vocal opponent to slavery, attacking the system that Jefferson, Madison, and

---

[8] Wallace, *The Long Bitter Trail*; White, *"It's Your Misfortune and None of My Own,"* 88-90.

Illustrations (left to right): Thomas Sully, *John Quincy Adams* (181);
Thomas Sully, *Andrew Jackson* (1845), ©Board of Trustees, National
Gallery of Art, Washington. Color plates, page 182.

Monroe had helped to defend. He also objected to the Removal Act,
condemning "the perfidy and tyranny of which the Indians are to be
made the victims, and leave the punishment of it to heaven."[9]

Adams' criticism of the Removal Act went hand-in-hand with his
rejection of territorial expansion. Adams shared the concerns of many
Americans who believed that expansion might tear the union apart.
Jefferson, Madison, and Monroe had agreed, so much so that in 1820
Monroe expressed his own belief that "further acquisition, of territory,
to the West & South, involves difficulties, of an internal nature, which
menace the Union itself. We ought therefore to be cautious in making
the attempt."[10] By the 1840's, however, most Americans had
undergone a change of mind. The very opportunities so many
Americans found in the land acquired through the Louisiana Purchase
played no small part in this change. When the United States went to
war with Mexico in 1846, Americans proclaimed expansion not only
beneficial, but also necessary to their survival as a nation.

---

[9] Quoted in Parsons, *John Quincy Adams*, 206.
[10] Monroe to Jefferson, May 1820, *Monroe Writings*, V: 11

This demand for territorial expansion would eventually be known as Manifest Destiny. It constituted a profound change from 1803, when Americans had expressed so many reservations about the expansion that came with the Louisiana Purchase. Adams could only marvel at the attitudes that prevailed in the 1840's and condemned the Mexican War from the House floor.

In the midst of one of these speeches in the House of Representatives, Adams suffered a stroke, dying two days later in the capital building where he had served so many years. Before the end of the year, the United States had reach an accord with Mexico, which transferred land that now constitutes the southwestern United States as well as California. That acquisition only intensified the debate over slavery begun by the Missouri Compromise. As one territory after another sought entry into the union, Americans repeatedly revisited the question of whether slavery would expand onto the western frontier. By 1861, the American constitutional structure could no longer accommodate the pressures it faced.[11]

The Louisiana Purchase obviously did not cause the Civil War by itself. Nor did the Louisiana Purchase create the angry debate over slavery. So how then should we consider the Louisiana Purchase in relation to American sectionalism? The answer recalls the central complexity of Louisiana's relationship to the United States, where it both shaped and reflected the nation's history. Considering the Louisiana Purchase together with the Civil War helps account for the *timing* of sectional discord. Statehood for the territories that had been part of Louisiana proved critical in shaping the trajectory of debate over the extension of slavery. The Louisiana Purchase shaped the contours of these debates, but did not create them.

In addition to extending the enslavement of African-Americans and propelling the sectional discord among whites, the Louisiana Purchase also proved to be a catalyst for the misery of North American Indians. The United States government exterminated Indians with a zeal and skill unmatched by the European empires that

---

[11] Gienapp, *The Origins of the Republican Party 1852-1856*; Holt, *The Political Crisis of the 1850s*, 2-4.

had occupied the Americas.

In the two centuries since 1803, the Louisiana Purchase would prove both beneficial and destructive depending on a person's background, circumstances, and goals. For example, while European immigrants found the abundance and freedom in the American West that was unobtainable in Europe, forced migration became a mournful reality for many Indians. Many tribes had made regional migration a regular part of their lives, often shifting among various hunting grounds or farming regions, but forced migration to unfamiliar soil meant permanent separation from familiar homes. At a more tangible level, the warfare and disease that had decimated Indian tribes in the East now descended on Indians in the West.

THE LOUISIANA PURCHASE AND THE UNITED STATES

By the end of the nineteenth century, textbooks and the first works of historical scholarship celebrated the Louisiana Purchase. In 1896 Theodore Roosevelt published a multi-volume history entitled *The Winning of the West*. Roosevelt had personal reasons for celebrating American expansion. The scion of a wealthy New York family, Roosevelt became a Dakota rancher in a desperate attempt to overcome his grief at the death of his first wife in 1884. Life in the West rejuvenated him, and it was no surprise that he saw in the West the story of America's greatest glory.

Roosevelt wrote that the "true history [of the Louisiana Purchase] is to be found, not in the doings of the diplomats who determined merely the terms upon which it was made, but the western growth of the people of the United States from 1769 to 1803, which made it inevitable." He added, "the men who settled and peopled the western wilderness were the men who won Louisiana; for it was surrendered by France merely because it was impossible to hold it against the American advance."[1]

Roosevelt's boisterous enthusiasm about American expansion extended beyond the boundaries of the Louisiana Purchase, and, for that matter, beyond North America itself. As assistant secretary of the navy, vice president, and then president, Roosevelt became an architect of American expansion across the Pacific. He considered the Louisiana Purchase part of a unifying and glorious story of American development. The Louisiana Purchase *did* open the gate for western expansion. At the same time, it came about for reasons having little to do with Roosevelt's narrative in *The Winning of the West*.

---

[1] Roosevelt, *The Winning of the West*, VI: 6.

A president with more historical training, Woodrow Wilson, understood that the Louisiana Purchase was indeed the product of "the doings of the diplomats." A professor at Princeton University, Wilson wrote a history of the United States soon after *The Winning of the West*. In it, he recalled the strange combination of circumstances that led to the Purchase.[2]

Despite their different analysis of events in 1803, both men nonetheless set the Purchase in a similar context. Their comments— and those of other men and women who celebrated the Purchase and the "winning" of the West —show a distinctive nineteenth-century perspective that assumed white Americans were entitled to the West. Novelists as well as historians believed that North America had indeed always been American, and the only intruders were the Indians. That Indians predated the arrival of white settlers often did not matter. Only in the late twentieth-century did Americans begin to reconsider their own past in ways that called into question the history of expansion.[3]

The varying perspectives that people have brought to the Louisiana Purchase reflect its complexity. Yet for all these agendas, certain things did remain consistent throughout this period.

Politics might have been the preserve of a small male elite, but it had profound ramifications for average Americans. White settlers enjoyed prosperity and a stable government that resolved their differences. African Americans remained enslaved because Congress and the administration endorsed the perpetuation of human bondage. Indians found their lives turned upside-down by American settlers who spread across the continent. Indians, slaves, and settlers could not have been further removed from the ornate rituals of negotiation in Washington and European capitals, but their lives depended on the outcome of international relations.

Finally, the Louisiana Purchase guaranteed that opportunity and conflict would be inseparable in the West. The Louisiana Purchase did indeed create new possibilities for millions of people. Settlers spoke

---

[2] Wilson, *History of the American People*, III: 183.
[3] Ann Fabian, "History for the Masses: Commercializing the Western Past," in Cronon, et. al, eds., *Under an Open Sky;* 223-38; Smith, *Virgin Land.*

about the hard work and adversity they faced, and they said that all this was possible only because that land was part of the United States. Their honesty contrasted with the honesty of slaves and Indians, who told the story of a Louisiana Purchase that opened the door for new forms of suffering and death.

Pulling together opinions so different is indeed the most difficult part of understanding the meaning of the Louisiana Purchase. It is also the most vital. That synthesis bridges the gap between a simple transfer of land and actual human experiences. It also connects a bill of sale to a nation's history.

Bibliography
Bibliographical Abbreviations

Document Repositories

HNO   Historic New Orleans Collection. New Orleans, Louisiana.

LC   Library of Congress. Washington, DC.

LSU   Special Collections, Hill Memorial Library, Louisiana State University. Baton Rouge, Louisiana.

NA   National Archives. Washington, DC.

NOPL   New Orleans Public Library. New Orleans, LA.

TUL   Special Collections, Howard-Tilton Memorial Library, Tulane University. New Orleans, Louisiana.

UVA   Special Collections, Alderman Library, University of Virginia. Charlottesville, VA.

Library of Congress

Jefferson Papers   *Thomas Jefferson Papers.* Microfilm Collection.

Madison Papers   *James Madison Papers.* Microfilm Collection.

Monroe Papers   *James Monroe Papers.* Microfilm Collection.

Rives Collection   *Rives Collection of Madison Papers.* Microfilm Collection.

National Archives

Consular Dispatches   *Dispatches from Consuls.* Record Group 59.

Letters Received, Registered Series   *Letters Received by the Secretary of War: Registered Series.* Record Group 107, Microfilm Copy M22.

Published Collections

Annals of Congress Debates and Proceedings of the Congress of the United States. Washington: Gales and Seaton, 1834-56, 42 vols.

ASP - American State Papers: Documents, Legislative and Executive, of the Congress of the United States. Washington: Gales and Seaton, 1832-61.

Boyd - *The Papers of Thomas Jefferson.* Julian Boyd, et. al., eds. Princeton: Princeton University Press, 1950-.

Carter - *The Territorial Papers of the United States.* Clarence Edward Carter, ed. Washington: Government Printing Office, 1934-1975, 28 vols.

Claiborne Letterbooks - The Letter Books of William C.C. Claiborne, 1801-1816. Dunbar Rowland, ed. Jackson: Mississippi State Library and Archive, 1917, 6 vols.

Ford - The Works of Thomas Jefferson. Paul Leicester Ford, ed. New York: G.P. Putnam's Sons, 1904-1905, 10 vols.

House Journal - Journal of the House of Representatives of the state of Louisiana. New Orleans: Thierry, Baird & Wagner, Peter K. Wagner, J.C. de St. Romes, 1812-1820.

Madison Writings - Letters and Other Writings of James Madison. New York: R. Worthington, 1884, 4 vols.

Monroe Writings - The Writings of James Monroe. Stanislaus Murray Hamilton, ed. New York: G.P. Putnam's Sons, 1898-1903, 7 vols.

PJM - The Papers of James Madison. William T. Hutchison, et. al., eds. Charlottesville and Chicago: University Press of Virginia and University of Chicago Press, 1962-91, 17 vols.

PJM-PS - The Papers of James Madison: Presidential Series. Robert A. Rutland, et. al., eds. Charlottesville: University Press of Virginia, 1986.

PJM-SS - The Papers of James Madison: Secretary of State Series. Robert J. Brugger, et. al., eds. Charlottesville: University Press of Virginia, 1986-, 3 vols to date.

Journals

JAH   *Journal of American History.*

JER   *Journal of the Early Republic.*

JSH   *Journal of Southern History.*

LAH   *Louisiana History.*

LHQ   *Louisiana Historical Quarterly.*

WMQ   *William and Mary Quarterly.*

Historical Documents and Document Collections

Adams, John Quincy. *Memoirs of John Quincy Adams, Comprising Portions of His Diary from 1795 to 1848.* Charles Francis Adams, ed. Philadelphia: J.B. Lippincott & Co., 1874.

Silbey, John. *A Topographical and Statistical Account of the Province of Louisiana &* Baltimore: Franklin Press, 1803.

An Account of Louisiana, Being an Abstract of Documents, in the Offices of the Departments of State, and of the Treasury. Washington: Duane, 1803, UVA.

le Page du Pratz, Antoine. *Histoire de la Louisiane...* Paris: De Bure, 1758, UVA.

Hennepin, Louis. *Description de la Louisiane...* Paris: Chez la Veuve Sebastien HurÉ, 1683, UVA.

Martin, Francois-Xavier. *A General Digest of the Acts of the Legislatures of the Late Territory of Orleans, and the State of Louisiana &* New Orleans: Peter K. Wagner, 1816.

Stiles, Henry Reed, ed. *Joutel's Journal of La Salle's Last Voyage, 1684-7.* Albany: J. McDonough, 1906.

Hutchins, Thomas. *An Historical Narrative and Topographical Description of Louisiana and West Florida.* Gainseville: University of Florida Press, 1968, UVA.

de Tonti, Henri, et. al, *On the Discovery of the Mississippi...* (London: S. Clark, 1844), UVA

Berquin-Duvallon. *Travels in Louisiana and the Floridas in the Year 1802.* New York: I. Riley & Co., 1806.

Brazer, Samuel. *Address, Pronounced at Worcester, on May 12th, 1804 in Commemoration of the Cession of Louisiana to the United States.* Worcester: Sewall Goodridge, 1804.

Duane, William. *The Mississippi question fairly stated &* Philadelphia: W. Duane, 1803

James F. Hopkins, et. al, eds. *The Papers of Henry Clay.* Lexington: University of Kentucky Press, 1959-.

Jackson, Donald, ed. *Letters of the Lewis and Clark Expedition, With Related Documents 1783-1854.* Urbana: University of Illinois Press, 1978.

The Journals of Zebulon Montgomery Pike. Norman: University of Oklahoma Press, 1966.

Kline, Mary-Jo, et. al, eds. *Political Correspondence and Public Papers of Aaron Burr.* Princeton: Princeton University Press, 2 vols., 1983.

Magruder, Allan Bowie. *Political, Commercial, and Moral Reflections on the Late Cession of Louisiana to the United States.* Lexington: D. Bradford, 1803.

Marshall, Thomas Maitland, ed. *The Life and Papers of Frederick Bates.* St. Louis: Missouri Historical Society, 1926.

Merrill, Orasmus Cook. *The Happiness of America. An Oration Delivered at Shaftsbury, on the Fourth of July, 1804.* Bennington: Anthony Haswell, 1804.

Robert L. Meriwether, et. al, eds. *The Papers of John C. Calhoun.* Columbia: University of South Carolina Press, 1959-.

Message from the President of the U. States, Transmitting the Constitution or Form of Government, Established by the Convention of the Territory of Orleans, for the Government of that Territory, when Erected into a Separate and Independent State, Under the title of The State of Louisiana. Washington: R.C. Weightman, 1812.

Peterson, Merrill D., ed. *The Portable Thomas Jefferson.* New York: Penguin Books, 1975.

Pitot, James. *Observations on the Colony of Louisiana from 1796 to 1802.* Baton Rouge: Louisiana State University Press, 1979.

Rakove, Jack N., ed. *James Madison: Writings.* New York: Library of America, 1999.

Ramsay, David. *An Oration on the Cession of Louisiana to the United States &* Charleston: W.P. Young, 1804.

Proceedings of the New Orleans Conseil de Ville. NOPL.

Reflections on the Cause of the Louisianians Respectfully Submitted by Their Agents.
Washington: 1803.

Smith, Sam B. and Harriet Chappell Owsley, et. al, eds. *The Papers of Andrew Jackson.* Knoxville: University of Tennessee Press, 1980-.

Tucker, St. George. *Reflections on the Cession of Louisiana to the United States.*
Washington City: Samuel Harrison Smith, 1803.

Newspapers

Alexandria [VA] Advertiser

Aurora and General Advertiser [Philadelphia, PA]

Charleston [SC] Courier

Connecticut Courant [Hartford]

Louisiana Courier [New Orleans]

Louisiana Gazette [New Orleans]

Moniteur de la Louisiane [New Orleans]

New York Evening Post.

Orleans Gazette [New Orleans]

Richmond [VA] Enquirer

Salem [MA] Gazette

St. Francisville [LA] Time Piece

Telegraphe [New Orleans]

Weekly Chronicle [Natchez, MS]

Articles

Allen, John L. "Geographical Knowledge & American Images of the Louisiana Territory." *Western Historical Quarterly* II (1971): 159-70.

DeGrummond, Jane Lucas. "Cayetana Susana Bosque y Fanqui: 'A Notable Woman.'" *LAH* XXII (1982): 277-94.

Dormon, James. "The Persistent Specter: Slave Rebellion in Territorial Louisiana." *LAH* XVIII (1977): 389-404

Freeman, Joanne B. "Dueling as Politics: Reinterpreting the Burr-Hamilton Duel." *WMQ*, 3d. ser. LIII (1996): 289-319.

"Slander, Poison, Whispers, and Fame: Jefferson's 'Anas' and Political Gossip in the Early Republic." *JER* XV (1995): 25-58.

Haggard, Villasana. "The Neutral Ground Between Louisiana and Texas, 1806-1821." *LHQ* XXVIII (1945): 1001-1128.

Holmes, Jack D. L. "Showdown on the Sabine: General James Wilkinson vs. Lieutenant-Colonel SimÛn de Herrera." *Louisiana Studies* III (1964): 46-76.

"The Abortive Slave Revolt at Pointe CoupÉe, Louisiana, 1795." *LAH* XI (1970): 341-62.

Holton, Woody. "The Ohio Indians and the Coming of the American Revolution in Virginia." *JSH* LX (1994): 453-79.

Ingersoll, Thomas N. "Free Blacks in a Slave Society: New Orleans, 1718-1812," *WMQ*, 3d. ser. XLVIII (1991): 173-200.

Kirkpatrick, R.L. "Professional, Religious, and Social Aspects of St. Louis Life, 1804-1816." *Missouri Historical Review* XLIV (1950): 373-86.

Kushner, Howard I. "The Suicide of Meriwether Lewis: A Psychological Inquiry." *WMQ*, 3d ser. 38 (1981): 464-81.

Lachance, Paul F. "The Politics of Fear: French Louisianans and the Slave Trade, 1786-1809." *Plantation Society* I (1979): 162-97.

Matthewson, Tim. "Jefferson and Haiti." *JSH* LXI (1995): 209-19.

McClesky, Turk. "Rich Land, Poor Prospects: Real Estate and the Formation of a Social elite in Augusta County, Virginia, 1738-1770." *The Virginia Magazine of History and Biography* LXLVIII (1990): 449-487.

Nobles, Gregory. "Straight Lines and Stability: Mapping the Political Order of the Anglo-American Frontier." *JAH* LXXX (1993): 9-35.

Onuf, Peter S. "'To Declare Them a Free and Independent People': Race, Slavery, and National Identity in Jefferson's Thought." *JER* XVIII (1998): 1-46.

Prichard, Walter. "Selecting a Governor for the Territory of Orleans." *LHQ* XXXI (1948): 269-393.

Stagg, J.C.A. "James Madison and the Coercion of Great Britain: Canada, the West Indies, and the War of 1812." *WMQ* 3d ser., XXXVIII (1981): 3-34.

"Summary of Trial Proceedings of those Accused of Participating in the Slave Uprising of January 9, 1811." *LAH* XVIII (1977): 472-3.

Taylor, Alan. "'The Art of Hook & Snivey:' Political Culture in Upstate New York During the 1790s." *JAH* LXXIX (1993): 1371-98.

Books, Theses, and Dissertations

Abernethy, Thomas Perkins. *The Burr Conspiracy.* Gloucester: Peter Smith, 1968

Allain, MathÉ. *"Not Worth a Straw": French Colonial Policy and the Early Years of Louisiana.* Lafayette: University of Southwestern Louisiana, 1988.

Ambrose, Stephen A. *Undaunted Courage: Meriwether Lewis, Thomas Jefferson, and the Opening of the American West.* New York: Simon & Schuster, 1996.

Ammon, Harry. *James Monroe: The Search for National Identity.* Charlottesville: University Press of Virginia, 1990.

Aptheker, Herbert. *American Negro Slave Revolts.* New York : International Publishers, 1974 [1933].

Aron, Stephen. *How the West was Lost: The Transformation of Kentucky from Daniel Boone to Henry Clay.* Baltimore: Johns Hopkins University Press, 1996.

Axtell, James. *Beyond 1492: Encounters in Colonial North America.* Oxford: Oxford University Press, 1992.

Bailyn, Bernard. *The Ideological Origins of the American Revolution*. Cambridge: Belknap Press, 1987 [1967].

Banning, Lance. *The Jeffersonian Persuasion: Evolution of a Party Ideology*. Ithaca: Cornell University Press, 1978.

The Sacred Fire of Liberty: James Madison & the Founding of the Federal Republic. Cornell: Cornell University Press, 1995.

Beeman, Richard, Stephen Botein, and Edward C. Carter, eds. *Beyond Confederation: Origins of the Constitution and American National Identity*. Chapel Hill: University of North Carolina Press, 1987.

Bell, Caryn CrossÉ. *Revolution, Romanticism, and the Afro-Creole Protest Tradition in Louisiana 1718-1868*. (Baton Rouge: Louisiana State University Press, 1997.

Biographical Directory of the United States Congress, 1774-1989. Washington: Government Printing Office, 1989.

Brasseaux, Carl A. *Denis-Nicolas Foucault and the New Orleans Rebellion of 1768*. Ruston: Louisiana Tech University, 1987.

Brown, Everett S. *The Constitutional History of the Louisiana Purchase*. Clifton: Augustus M. Kelley, 1972 [1920].

Brown, Stuart Gerry, ed. *The Autobiography of James Monroe*. Syracuse: Syracuse University Press, 1959.

Cayton, Andrew R. L. *The Frontier Republic: Ideology and Politics in The Ohio Country*. Kent: Kent State University Press, 1986.

Clarke, Charles G. *The Men of the Lewis and Clark Expedition: A Biographical Roster of the Fifty-One Members and a Composite Diary of their Activities from all Known Sources*. Glendale: Arthur H. Clark, 1970.

Cox, Isaac. *The West Florida Controversy, 1798-1813: A Study in American Diplomacy*. Baltimore: Johns Hopkins University Press, 1923.

Crackel, Theodore J. *Mr. Jefferson's Army: Political and Social Reform of the Military Establishment, 1801-1809*. New York: New York University Press, 1987.

Cronon, William, George Miles, and Jay Gitlin, eds. *Under an Open Sky: Rethinking America's Western Past*. New York: Norton, 1992.

Dangerfield, George. *Chancellor Robert R. Livingston of New York, 1746-1813*. New York: Harcourt, Brace, 1960.

Dargo, George. *Jefferson's Louisiana: Politics and the Clash of Legal Traditions*. Cambridge: Harvard University Press, 1975.

DeConde, Alexander. *This Affair of Louisiana*. New York: Charles Scribner's Sons, 1976.

Deen, Isabelle Claxton. "Public Response to the Louisiana Purchase: A Survey of American Press and Pamphlets, 1801-1804." Charlottesville: MA Thesis, University of Virginia, 1972.

Din, Gilbert C. and Harkins, John E. *The New Orleans Cabildo: Colonial Louisiana's First City Government 1769-1803*. Baton Rouge: Louisiana State University Press, 1996.

Dobyns, Henry F. *Their Number Become Thinned: Native American Population Dynamics in Eastern North America.* Knoxville: University of Tennessee Press, 1983.

Dowd, Gregory. *A Spirited Resistance: The North American Indian Struggle for Unity.* Baltimore: Johns Hopkins University Press, 1992.

Ekberg, Carl J. *'Colonial Ste. Genevieve: An Adventure on the Mississippi Frontier.* Gerald: The Patrice Press, 1985.

Flores, Dan. *Jefferson & Southwestern Exploration: The Freeman & Custis Accounts of the Red River Expedition of 1806.* Norman: University of Oklahoma Press, 1984.

Foley, William E. *The Genesis of Missouri: From Wilderness Outpost to Statehood.* Columbia: University of Missouri Press, 1989.

GayarrÉ, Charles E.A. *History of Louisiana.* New Orleans: F.F. Hansell & Bro., Ltd., 4 vols., 1903 [1854-66].

Gienapp, William E. *The Origins of the Republican Party 1852-1856.* Oxford and New York: Oxford University Press, 1987.

Haas, Edward F., Jr., ed. *Louisiana's Legal Heritage.* Pensacola: Perdido Bay Press, 1983.

Hall, Gwendolyn Midlo. *Africans in Colonial Louisiana: The Development of Afro-Creole Culture in the Eighteenth Century.* Baton Rouge: Louisiana State University Press, 1992.

Hanger, Kimberly S. *Bounded Lives, Bounded Places: Free Black Society in Colonial New Orleans, 1769-1803.* Durham: Duke University Press, 1997.

Hatfield, Joseph T. *William Claiborne: Jeffersonian Centurion in the American Southwest.* Lafayette: University of Southwestern Louisiana, 1976.

Hirsch, Arnold R. and Joseph Logsdon, eds. Creole *New Orleans: Race and Americanization.* Baton Rouge: Louisiana State University Press, 1992.

Holt, Michael. *The Political Crisis of the 1850s.* New York: Norton, 1978.

Jackson, Donald T. *Thomas Jefferson & the Stony Mountain: Exploring the West from Monticello.* Urbana: University of Illinois Press, 1981.

John, Richard R. *Spreading the News: The American Postal System from Franklin to Morse.* Cambridge: Harvard University Press, 1995.

Kaplan, Lawrence S. *Entangling Alliances with None: American Foreign Policy in the Age of Jefferson.* Kent: Kent State University Press, 1987.

Ketcham, Ralph. *James Madison: A Biography.*† Charlottesville: University Press of Virginia, 1990 [1971].

Langley, Lester. *The Americas in the Age of Revolution.* New Haven: Yale University Press, 1996.

Lewis, James E., Jr. *The American Union and the Problem of Neighborhood: The United States and the Collapse of the Spanish Empire, 1783-1829.* Chapel Hill: University of North Carolina Press, 1998.

Lyon, E. Wilson. *The Man Who Sold Louisiana: The Career of Francois Barbé-Marbois.* Norman: University of Oklahoma Press, 1942.

Maier, Pauline. *American Scripture: Making the Declaration of Independence.* New York: Knopf, 1997.

Malone, Dumas, ed., *Correspondence Between Thomas Jefferson and Pierre Samuel du Pont de Nemours 1798-1817.* Boston: Houghton Mifflin Company, 1930.

Malone, Dumas. *Jefferson the Virginian.* New York: Little Brown, 1948.

McCaleb, Walter Falvius. *The Aaron Burr Conspiracy.* New York: Argosy-Antiquarian Press, 1966.

McConnell, Roland C. *Negro Troops of Antebellum Louisiana: A History of the Battalion of Free Men of Color.* Baton Rouge: Louisiana State University Press, 1968.

McCoy, Drew R. *The Elusive Republic: Political Economy in Jeffersonian America.* New York: Norton.

The Last of the Fathers: James Madison & the Republican Legacy (Cambridge: Cambridge University Press, 1988)

Moore, Glover. *The Missouri Controversy, 1819-1821.* Lexington: University of Kentucky Press, 1953.

Moore, John Preston. *Revolt in Louisiana: the Spanish Occupation, 1766-1770.* Baton Rouge: Louisiana State University Press, 1976.

Muhlstein, Anka. *La Salle: Explorer of the North American Frontier.* Willard Wood, trans. New York: Arcade Publishing, 1994.

Nasatir, Abraham. *Borderland in Retreat: From Spanish Louisiana to the Far Southwest.* Albuquerque: University of New Mexico Press, 1976.

Onuf, Peter S. *Statehood and Union: A History of the Northwest Ordinance.* Bloomington: Indiana University Press, 1987.

The *Origins of the Federal Republic: Jurisdictional Controversies in the United States, 1775-1787.* Philadelphia: University of Pennsylvania Press, 1983.

Onuf, Peter S. and Nicholas G. Onuf. *Federal Union, Modern World: The Law of Nations in an Age of Revolutions, 1776-1814.* Madison: Madison House, 1993.

Onuf, Peter S. ed. *Jeffersonian Legacies.* Charlottesville: University Press of Virginia, 1993.

Perkins, Bradford. *Castlereagh and Adams: England and the United States, 1812-1823.* Berkeley: University of California Press, 1964.

Prologue to War: England and the United States, 1805-1812. Berkeley, University of California Press, 1961.

Peterson, Merrill D. *The Great Triumvirate: Webster, Clay, and Calhoun.* Oxford: Oxford University Press, 1987.

Thomas Jefferson and the New Nation: A Biography. Oxford: Oxford University Press, 1970.

Price, Edward T. *Dividing the Land: Early American Beginnings of Our Private Property Mosaic.* Chicago: University of Chicago Press, 1995.

Prucha, Francis Paul. *American Indian Policy in the Formative Years: The Indian Trade and Intercourse Acts.* Cambridge: Harvard University Press, 1962.

Rakove, Jack N. *James Madison and the Creation of the American Republic.* New York: Harper Collins, 1990.

Original Meanings: Politics and Ideas in the Making of the Constitution. New York: Vintage.

Ramenofsky, Ann F. *Vectors of Death: The Archaeology of European Contact.* Albuquerque: University of New Mexico Press, 1987.

Romero, Sidney J. *"My Fellow Citizens & ": The Inaugural Addresses of Louisiana's Governors.* Lafayette: University of Southwestern Louisiana, 1980.

Roosevelt, Theodore. *The Winning of the West.* New York: The Current Literature Publishing Company, 1905.

Sellers, Charles. *The Market Revolution: Jacksonian America, 1815-1846.* New York : Oxford University Press, 1991.

Sheehan, Bernard W. *Seeds of Extinction: Jeffersonian Philanthropy and the American Indian.* Chapel Hill: University of North Carolina Press 1973.

Shoemaker, F.C. *'Missouri's Struggle for Statehood 1804-1821.* Jefferson City: The Hugh Stephens Printing Co., 1916.

Slaughter, Thomas P. *The Whiskey Rebellion: Frontier Epilogue to the American Revolution.* Oxford and New York: Oxford University Press, 1986.

Sloan, Herbert E. *Principle and Interest: Thomas Jefferson and the Problem of Debt.* New York, Oxford: Oxford University Press, 1995.

Smith, F. Todd. *The Caddo Indians: Tribes at the Convergence of Empires, 1542-1854.* College Station: Texas A&M Press, 1995.

Smith, Henry Nash. *Virgin Land: The American West as Symbol and Myth.* Cambridge: Harvard University Press, 1970 [1950].

Spivak, Burton. *Jefferson's English Crisis: Commerce, Embargo, and the Republican Revolution.* Charlottesville: University Press of Virginia, 1979.

Stagg, J.C.A. *Mr. Madison's War: Politics, Diplomacy, and Warfare in the Early American Republic, 1783-1830.* Princeton: Princeton University Press, 1983.

Taylor, Alan. *Liberty Men and Great Proprietors: The Revolutionary Settlement on the Maine Frontier, 1760-1820.* Chapel Hill: University of North Carolina Press, 1990.

William Cooper's Town: Power and Persuasion on the Frontier of the Early American Republic. New York: Norton, 1995.

Texada, David Ker. *Alejandro O'Reilly and the New Orleans Rebels.* Lafayette: Southwestern Louisiana State University Press, 1970.

Thornton, Russell. *American Indian Holocaust and Survival: A Population History since 1492.* Norman: University of Oklahoma Press, 1987.

Tucker, Robert W. and Hendrickson, David C. *Empire of Liberty: The Statecraft of Thomas Jefferson*. New York: Oxford University Press, 1990.

Usner, Daniel H. Jr. *Indians, Settlers, & Slaves in a Frontier Exchange Economy*. Chapel Hill: University of North Carolina Press, 1992.

Villeré, Sidney Louis. *Jacques Philippe Villeré, First Native-Born Governor of Louisiana, 1816-1820*. New Orleans: Historic New Orleans Collection, 1981.

Wallace, Anthony. *The Long Bitter Trail: Andrew Jackson and the Indians*. New York: Hill and Wang, 1993.

Walters, Ray. *Albert Gallatin: Jeffersonian Financier and Diplomat*. Pittsburgh: University of Pittsburgh Press, 1969.

Weber, David J. *The Spanish Frontier in North America*. New Haven: Yale University Press, 1992.

Weeks, William Earl. *John Quincy Adams and American Global Empire*. Lexington: University Press of Kentucky, 1992.

White, Leonard. *The Jeffersonians: A Study in Administrative History 1801-1829*. New York: Macmillan, 1951.

White, Richard. *"It's Your Misfortune and None of My Own": A New History of the American West*. Norman: University of Oklahoma Press, 1991.

The Middle Ground: Indians, Empires, and Republics in the Great Lakes Region, 1650-1815. Cambridge: Cambridge University Press, 1991.

Williams, R.G., ed. *Iberville's Gulf Journals*. University: University of Alabama Press, 1981.

Wilson, Woodrow. *History of the American People*. New York: Harper & Brothers, 1906.

Wood, Gordon S. *The Radicalism of the American Revolution*. New York: Knopf, 1992.

Young, James Sterling. *The Washington Community 1800-1828*. New York: Columbia University Press, 1966.

INDEX

Illustration: Jean Baptiste Michel Le Bouteaux, *View of the Campe of the Concession of Monseigneur Law at New Biloxi, Coast of Louisiana* (1710), Courtesy of the Edward E. Ayer Collection, Newberry Library, Chicago.

COLOR PLATES

167

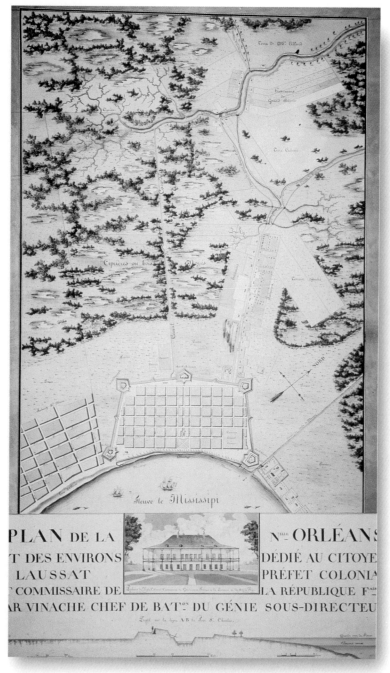

Joseph Antoine Vinache, *Plan de la Nouvelle Orléans et des Environs Dedié au Citoyen Laussat Préfet Colonial et Commissaire de la République FranÁaise* Courtesy of the Historic New Orleans Collection, accession no. 1987.65

Illustrations (left to right): Top: John Trumbull, *John Adams* (1793), National Portrait Gallery, Smithsonian Institution; Middle: Gilbert Stuart, *George Washington* (c. 1821); John Trumbull, *Alexander Hamilton* (1806); Bottom: Gilbert Stuart, *James Madison* (c. 1821),©Board of Trustees, National Gallery of Art, Washington.

Gilbert Stuart, *Thomas Jefferson* (c. 1821) National Portrait Gallery,
Smithsonian Institution

COLOR PLATES

Jacques-Louis David, *Napoleon in His Study* (1812), © Board of Trustees, National Gallery of Art, Washington.

Illustrations (left to right) Top: Francois Barbé-Marbois, from the collections of Louisiana State Museum; John Vanderlyn, *James Monroe* (1816), National Portrait Gallery, Smithsonian Institution; Bottom: John Vanderlyn, *Robert R. Livingston* (1804), collection of the New York Historical Society.

Illustrations: subsequent renderings of the final arrangements for the Louisiana Purchase. Top: Napoleon dictates plans for the Purchase to his ministers, Historic New Orleans Collection, accession no. 1974.25.10.64 Bottom: American and French diplomats sign the treaty, Historic New Orleans Collection, accession no. 1974.25.10.65.

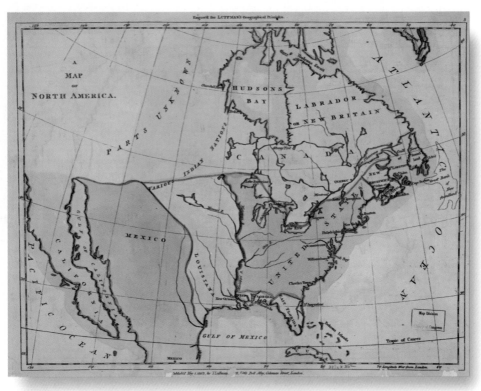

Illustrations: John Luffman, *A Map of North America*, (London: 1803),
Geography and Map Division, courtesy of the Library of Congress

COLOR PLATES

Joseph Marx Liechtenstern, *Nord America mit Benützung der neuesten and zuverlaessigsten Quellen und Hülfsmittel*, (1804). John Luffman's 1803 map used vague geographic references to indicate the boundaries of the United States, Louisiana, and Mexico. Liechtenstern's map provided a more detailed description of landscape, but with only a single line to indicate the western boundary of Louisiana and no northern terminus. Geography and Map Division, Library of Congress

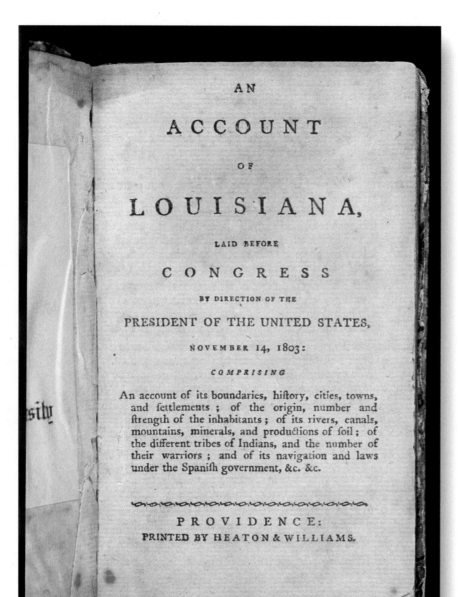

AN

ACCOUNT

OF

LOUISIANA,

LAID BEFORE

CONGRESS

BY DIRECTION OF THE

PRESIDENT OF THE UNITED STATES,

NOVEMBER 14, 1803:

COMPRISING

An account of its boundaries, hiſtory, cities, towns, and ſettlements ; of the origin, number and ſtrength of the inhabitants ; of its rivers, canals, mountains, minerals, and productions of ſoil ; of the different tribes of Indians, and the number of their warriors ; and of its navigation and laws under the Spaniſh government, &c. &c.

PROVIDENCE:

PRINTED BY HEATON & WILLIAMS.

Illustration: From An Account of Louisiana (Providence: Heaton & Williams, 1803), courtesy of Special Collections, Washington University in St. Louis.

Illustration: Charles Wilson Peale, *William Clark* (1810), Independence
National Historical Park;

Illustration: Charles Wilson Peale, *Meriwether Lewis,* Independence National Historical Park

COLOR PLATES

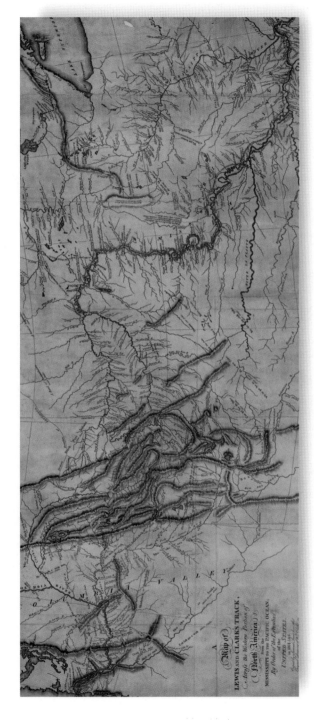

Illustration: William Clark, *A Map of Lewis and Clark's Track*(1814), courtesy of the Library of Congress.

Illustration: The transfer of Louisiana from France to the United States,
Thure De Thulstrup, Louisiana Historical Society. Image courtesy of the
Louisiana State Museum.

Illustrations (top to bottom): Charles Wilson Peale, *James Wilkinson*, Independence National Historical Park; Charles Wilson Peale, *Zebulon Pike*, Independence National Historical Park;

Illustrations (top): John Vanderlyn, *Aaron Burr* (1809), New York Historical Society; (bottom, left to right): Thomas Sully, *John Quincy Adams* (181); Thomas Sully, *Andrew Jackson* (1845), ©Board of Trustees, National Gallery of Art, Washington.